Individual Applicatic

T0153868

Prof. Dr. Erdal Tercan

Individual Application in Turkish Law

Universitätsverlag Regensburg

Entwicklungen im Europäischen Recht
Developments in European Law
Développements en droit européen

Herausgegeben von Rainer Arnold

Vol. 5

Bibliografische Information der Deutschen Nationalbibliothek
Die Deutsche Nationalbibliothek verzeichnet diese Publikation in der Deutschen
Nationalbibliografie; detaillierte bibliografische Daten sind im Internet über
http://dnb.dnb.de abrufbar.

1. Auflage 2015
© 2015 Universitätsverlag, Regensburg
Leibnizstraße 13, 93055 Regensburg
Umschlaggestaltung: Anna Braungart, Tübingen
Layout: Vollnhals Fotosatz, Neustadt a. d. Donau
Druck: Docupoint, Magdeburg
ISBN 978-3-86845-121-4

Weitere Informationen zum Verlagsprogramm erhalten Sie unter:
www.universitaetsverlag-regensburg.de

Content

Foreword

Primacy of the Constitution and the efficient protection of the individual by fundamental rights are the main pillars of Rule of Law in modern constitutionalism. Constitutional justice is its primordial guardian. The individual application is the procedural link between Constitution and the person.

In Germany, the *Verfassungsbeschwerde* is highly appreciated as an expression of the new, anthropocentric orientation under the *Grundgesetz* and has significantly contributed to the development of constitutional law. In Turkey, the individual application created in 2010 is of great importance. It is of high interest to analyze its nature, function and purpose as well as the procedural issues connected with this institution.

Professor Dr. Erdal Tercan, Judge at the Constitutional Court of the Republic of Turkey and excellent expert in constitutional law, gives a profound insight into structure and function of this new constitutional remedy.

Rainer Arnold

Introduction

Although human rights may differ from time to time and from one country to another, they define the rights that an individual possesses for being a person *per se*. In the result of the developments in scientific and philosophical thoughts throughout the history of mankind, it has been generally agreed and accepted that all people, regardless of their positions, have certain inalienable rights and that they must enjoy these rights without being exposed to any kind of discrimination. However, this result was not achieved easily.

How the states treat their citizens was regarded as an internal affair of the states themselves until the beginning of the World War II. There have been two interrelated positive developments after the World War II in the twentieth century which is accepted to be one of the bloodiest time periods in human history and which also witnessed numerous inhumane treatments. Firstly, the concept of human rights has been introduced to positive international law and universal protection of human rights has become an item of international agenda. Secondly, the idea that the constitutionality of the acts of the parliaments who were not thought to violate their own citizens' rights must be reviewed by an independent body has gained recognition[1].

Many authors indicate to "ensuring the constitutionality of laws" or "the protection of constitutional order" as the reason for the emergence of constitutional jurisdiction. Nevertheless, the protection of fundamental rights and freedoms must also be recognized as another basic function of the constitutional jurisdiction. Although the function of the constitutional jurisdiction to protect fundamental rights and freedoms was considered to be of secondary nature in the past, the function to protect fundamental rights and freedoms is the most distinctive feature of the contemporary constitutional courts and high courts with the capacity to serve the functions of constitutional courts. The mechanism of individual application, or constitutional complaint, constitutes the top level of development attained by the constitutional jurisdiction in protecting the fundamental rights. Although the practices vary in every country, most of the states have accorded its citizens the right to demand direct protection from the constitutional courts when their fundamental rights are violated by acts of public power. Although such mechanism has been discussed in our country since 1960s, constitutional complaint or individual application has not been included in legal protection methods. The Constitutional Court could only be referred for abstract or concrete review of norms. Whereas the individuals were not granted the right to make such an application directly, Turkish constitutional law had known and discussed individual application as a means of the constitutional complaint only through the practices of other countries.[2]

There has been discussion both in doctrine and practice on whether to adopt this legal remedy into Turkish Law. Whether the adoption of individual application would relieve the

---

1   Kılınç, Bahadır: Federal Almanya'da Bireysel Başvuru (Anayasa Şikayeti) Yolu: Anayasa Mahkemesi'ne Bireysel Başvuru Hakkı Sempozyumu, 26 Kasım 2010, Eskişehir 2011, p. 87.

2   Öcal, Saniye: Die Einführung der Verfassungsbeschwerde Als Neues Recht In der Türkei: Eine Besserstellung zum Schutz der Grund-Freiheitsrechte? : Yedi Tepe Üniversitesi Hukuk Fakültesi Dergisi, C.VII/1, 2010, p. 214.

workload of the courts or not has also been discussed. The objective of better protection of human rights and reducing the number of applications against Turkey filed with the European Court of Human Rights (ECtHR), the good examples in other countries and the successful results achieved with constitutional complaint in such countries as Germany and Spain revealed the need for the adoption of individual application in Turkish law as well.

Individual application was introduced to our legal system with the amendment of Article 148 of the Constitution and the inclusion of this right to mentioned Article as a part of the constitutional amendments approved by referendum on 12 September 2010. Individual application was included in the Constitution through Article 18 of the Law Nr. 5982 and I would like to quote some parts of the reasoning for the adoption of individual application: "....

When we look at the situation of Turkey, we see that individual application mechanism is not adopted but right to individual application to the European Court of Human Rights and the compulsory jurisdiction of this Court is recognized. It has been accepted that the complaints for the violation of fundamental rights which are not solved in domestic law shall be handled at supranational level through the European Court of Human Rights. Numerous cases are filed against Turkey before the European Court of Human Rights each year and Turkey is sentenced to pay compensation in many cases.

While examining the exhaustion of all domestic remedies, the European Court of Human Rights takes account of whether the individual application mechanism is implemented in the relevant country or not, and considers it to be an effective legal remedy in eliminating the violation of rights. Therefore, with the introduction of individual application mechanism, it is considered that a significant number of those alleging to be victims of violation of rights will be satisfied at individual application stage, namely before applying to the European Court of Human Rights, and that the number of cases to be filed and the decisions of violation to be rendered against Turkey will reduce. In this respect, establishment of a well-functioning individual application mechanism in Turkey will improve the standards on the basis of rights and rule of law.

......

The introduction of individual application mechanism in Turkey will ensure better protection of the fundamental rights and freedoms of individuals on one hand, and force the public organs to abide by the Constitution and laws on the other hand. With the amendment made to that end, the citizens are entitled the right to individual application and Constitutional Court is assigned the duty to examine and rule on such applications for the protection and guaranteeing of individual rights and freedoms.

......"3.

Therefore, the examination of the individual applications has been included into the duties of the Constitutional Court, as is the case in many other European countries.[4]

Article 148 of the Constitution regulates the individual application and paragraphs 3, 4 and 5 of the mentioned Article read as follows: "*Everyone may apply to the Constitutional Court on the grounds that one of the fundamental rights and freedoms within the scope of the European Conven-*

---

3   www: tbmm.gov.tr/sirasayi/dönem23/yıl01/ss497ek1. (Internet Access Date (IAD): 04.08.2012)

4   For instance, Albania, Armenia, Austria, Azerbaijan, Belgium, Bosnia Herzigovina, Croatia, Cyprus, Czech Republic, Georgia, Germany, Hungary, Latvia, Liechtenstein, Malta, Montenegro, Poland, Serbia, Slovenia, Spain, Switzerland, to a certain degree, Cyprus, Macedonia and Slovakia

tion on Human Rights which are guaranteed by the Constitution has been violated by public au-
thorities. In order to make an application, ordinary legal remedies shall be exhausted. – In the indi-
vidual application, the matters required to be taken into account during the process of (ordinary)
legal remedies shall not be reviewed. - Procedures and principles concerning the individual applica-
tion shall be regulated by law."

With respect to this amendment in our Constitution, the mechanism of individual application has been regulated in details in the Law Nr. 6216 dated 30.03.2011 on the Establishment
and Rules of Procedure of the Constitutional Court of Turkey (CCL) (Art. 45-51). Likewise,
the remaining aspects of the issue are regulated in details in the Internal Regulations of the
Constitutional Court, which entered into force upon publishing in the Official Gazette on 12
July 2012.

In accordance with Article 76 of the CCL, the Articles 45-51 regulating the individual application entered into force on 23.09.2012.

With the adoption of individual application mechanism, there have been significant
changes in the assigned duties of the Constitutional Court. From now on, the Constitutional
Court will devote most of its labor to the protection of human rights against the acts of public power. Although the Court's scope of review was limited only with the legislative acts before the individual application, it has expanded to cover acts of the executive and judiciary
with the introduction of individual application mechanism. Similarly, the adoption of individual application mechanism brought changes in the nature of the review carried by the
Constitutional Court. While the primary function of the Court before the adoption of individual application was to carry out the constitutionality review of the abstract norms upon
annulment or exception actions, after this amendment it will be obliged to devote most of its
labor to examine whether the fundamental rights of the individuals have been violated or not
in concrete cases.

The adoption of individual application mechanism has brought out two major matters to
be coped with by the Court. One of them is about the content of the decisions to be given by
the Court. The decisions to be given by the Court relating to individual application cases
should be such as to answer the modern needs in the protection of fundamental rights or they
should be parallel to the case-law of the ECtHR at least. The second one is that, although it is
impossible to foresee the actual size as from today, how the Court will cope with the workload
problem that none doubts to be immense[5]. The Court's performance on these two issues will
also be decisive in whether the ECtHR will recognize the individual application as an effective
remedy or not.[6]

---

[5] Çoban, Ali Rıza: Yeni Anayasa Mahkemesi Kanunu'nun Mahkemenin İş Yüküne Etkisi Açısından Değerlendirilmesi:
     "Bireysel Başvuru, Anayasa Şikayeti": HUKAB Sempozyum Serisi 1, 13 Mayıs 2011, p. 162 vd.
[6] The European Court of Human Rights recognised in Hasan Uzun v. Turkey that individual application in Tur-
     key is, in principle, effective and a remedy to be exhausted.

§.1 – Concept of individual application, its definition, nature and purpose

A – Concept of individual application

In Turkish law doctrine, previously the concept of "constitutional complaint" was used with reference to the concept of "Verfassungsbeschwerde" used in the German Law.[6]. Similarly, there is a distinction of "real constitutional complaint" and "unreal constitutional complaint" in the doctrine[7]. In technical terms, an application made in case of the violation of rights and freedoms regulated in the Constitution with a view to prevent such violation is called right of constitutional complaint, whereas the right granted to individuals to apply to the Constitutional Court for any other reasons is not accepted to be constitutional complaint[8]. In this sense, as the individual application mechanism ensures the individuals' application to Constitutional Court with the view to protect the fundamental rights and freedoms regulated in the constitution, it would be appropriate to use term "constitutional complaint" both in technical or actual sense.

However, Austrian law uses "Individualantrag" which means "individual demand, application", French law uses "requête individuelle" which may be translated as individual application; and the Spanish law uses "Recurso de amparo" which means application for protection[9]. Venice Commission uses both the term "constitutional complaint" and the term "Individual Application". Similarly, the term individual application is used in applying to the ECtHR for the protection of fundamental rights and freedoms[10]. The term "individual application" is used explicitly both in Article 148 of our Constitution and Article 45 of the CCL, thus, the term is regulated at constitutional and legal level. While the term "individual application" is preferred in the Constitution and the CCL, foreign laws may have adopted other terms used to that end as it is described above. Furthermore, the use of term "individual application" also suits the fact that the individuals can not use other means of application, especially annulment or exception actions, to the Constitutional Court in our legal system, and that there is no previously existing application mechanism for the violation of fundamental rights and freedoms; and that the individuals themselves can apply individually to the Court for the protection of their own rights and freedoms with adoption of this mechanism.

---

6   Göztepe, Ece: Anayasa Şikayeti, Ankara 1998, p. 15 vd. (Göztepe-Şikayet); Pekcanıtez, Hakan: Mukayeseli Hukukta Medeni Yargıda Verilen Kararlara Karşı Anayasa Şikayeti: Anayasa Yargısı 12, Ankara 1995, p. 257 vd.; Özbey, Özcan: Türk Hukukunda Anayasa Mahkemesine Bireysel Başvuru Hakkı, 2.B., Ankara 2013, p. 65-66; Aliyev, Cabir: Anayasa Şikayeti, İstanbul 2010, p. 7 vd.

7   Sağlam, Fazıl: Anayasa Şikayeti Kurumunun Türk Hukukuna Kazandırılması ile İlgili Sorunlar ve Çözüm Olanakları: Anayasa Yargısı İncelemeleri 1, Ankara 2006, p. 101 vd.

8   Göztepe Ece: Türkiye'de Anayasa Mahkemesi'ne Bireysel Başvuru Hakkının (Anayasa Şikayeti) 6216 Sayılı Kanun Kapsamında Değerlendirilmesi: Türkiye Barolar Birliği Dergisi 2011 (95), p. 17,19. (Göztepe-Değerlendirme)

9   Esen Arnwine, Selin: İspanya'da Amparo Başvurusu ve Türkiye: Anayasa Mahkemesi'ne Bireysel Başvuru Hakkı Sempozyumu, 26 Kasım 2010, Eskişehir 2011, p. 100.

10 Kılınç, p. 88.

For the grounds mentioned above, in this study we prefer the term "individual application" as it is used in Article 148 of the Constitution, Article 45 and forthcoming Articles of the CCL.

B – Definition and legal nature of the individual application

To ensure a better understanding of the individual application mechanism, it would be appropriate to make a definition of it in the first place and to determine its legal nature accordingly.

I – Definition

The individual application is not defined in the Constitution or in the CCL. However, Article 45, paragraph I of the CCL includes the provision of *"Every person may apply to the Constitutional Court alleging that the public power has violated any one of his/her fundamental rights and freedoms secured under the Constitution which falls into the scope of the European Convention on Human Rights and additional protocols thereto, to which Turkey is a party."* A similar provision is also present in Article 148, III of the Constitution. Although this provision does not define the individual application mechanism explicitly, it includes most of the aspects to be covered in the definition.

The grounds for the provision in Article 148, III of the Constitution includes such a definition: *"Individual application or the constitutional complaint is defined as an extraordinary legal remedy that individuals whose fundamental rights and freedoms have been violated by a public power may appeal to."* Some of the definitions in the doctrine are as follows: *"Individual application can be defined as an extraordinary legal remedy that the individuals whose fundamental rights and freedoms have been violated by the acts of legislative, executive and judiciary organs may appeal to"*[11]. Another definition is: *"Individual application can be defined as an extraordinary legal remedy that individuals whose fundamental rights and freedoms have been violated by a public power may appeal to"*[12]. Another definition says: *"Individual application is an exceptional and extraordinary legal remedy that allows the individuals under certain conditions to demand the intervention of constitutional judges for the protection of his/her constitutional rights against the acts of the executive and the judiciary"*[13]. The number of examples may be increased.

Taking into account such factors as who are entitled to individual application, what the subject matters of application are and where the applications are filed to, the individual application can be defined as follows within the framework of the provisions of Article 148, paragraph III of the Constitution and Article 45, paragraph I of the CCL: **Individual application is an extraordinary legal remedy which allows for the individuals whose fundamental rights and freedoms secured under the Constitution which falls into the scope of the Euro-**

---

[11] Kılınç p. 90.

[12] Atasoy, Hakan: Türk Hukukunda Bireysel Başvuru Yolu: Türkiye Adalet Akademisi Dergisi, Yıl:3, Sayı:9, Nisan 2012, p. 72.

[13] Sağlam, Musa: Bir Hak Arama Yolu Olarak Bireysel Başvuru: Anayasa Mahkemesi'ne Bireysel Başvuru Hakkı Sempozyumu, 26 Kasım 2010, Eskişehir 2011, p. 29, (Sağlam – Bireysel Başvuru).

pean Convention on Human Rights (and additional protocols thereto, to which Turkey is a party) have been violated by a public power, to apply to the Constitutional Court for the elimination of such violations.

II – Legal Nature

The first question to be emphasized as regards to the legal nature of the individual application is whether it is a lawsuit or not, and the second question is to determine its characteristics in terms of appeal ways and legal remedy.

Is the individual application a lawsuit or is it a kind of lawsuit? Can we use the term "lawsuit" for the individual application?

It must be stated in the first place that Article 50, paragraph V of the CCL includes the provision of *"Decision of dismissal shall be given in case of withdrawal of the lawsuit"*[14]. Likewise, according a view in doctrine, individual application is a kind of lawsuit which allows for the individuals, whose fundamental rights and freedoms have been violated, to appeal to the courts in charge of protecting such rights[15].

Generally, lawsuit is defined in the civil procedure law as follows: *"Lawsuit is the request of legal protection from the courts by the persons whose rights have been violated or jeopardized by others, for the elimination of such violation or jeopardy in an indisputable and prospective fashion"*[16]. As it is known, the party to file the lawsuit is called plaintiff and the party against whom the lawsuit is filed is called defendant. Therefore, the existence of two separate parties as the plaintiff and the defendant is a *sine qua non* for the lawsuit. When we look at the individual application in this respect, although there is an applicant who may be considered to be a plaintiff, there is not an opposing party to be considered as defendant. Although the provision of *"In case an individual application is declared admissible, a copy of the application is notified to the Ministry of Justice. The Ministry of Justice submits their opinion if they deem it necessary"* is included Article 49, paragraph II of the CCL, such submissions of the Ministry of Justice do not set the Ministry to the position of one of the parties or the defendant position. Therefore, as there is no party in defendant position, it can not be mentioned of lawsuit in this case. Yet again, as there are no two contesting parties, it can not be mentioned of an adversarial lawsuit as well. Therefore, in my opinion, it is not appropriate to use the term "lawsuit" in technical terms for the individual application mechanism[17].

---

14 Clause a and b in Paragraph 1 of Article 80 of the Internal Regulations includes the concept of "case" and quotes as "a) Explicit withdrawal of the applicant from the case, b) Understanding that the applicant has dismissed his/her case proceedingp."

15 Atasoy p. 73. "Constiutional complaint is a type of case within the constitutional jurisdiction like abstratct or concrete norm review" Göztepe-Şikayet p. 15, dn.35.; Armağan, Servet: Federal Almanya'da Anayasa Şikayeti, Mukayeseli Hukuk Araştırmaları Dergisi, C.7, Ayrı Bası, İstanbul 1971, p. 8, dn.18.

16 Pekcanıtez, Hakan / Atalay, Oğuz / Özekes, Muhammet: Medenî Usul Hukuku, 12. B., Ankara 2011, p. 289; Aynı yönde diğer bir tanım için bkz: Kuru, Baki / Arslan, Ramazan /Yılmaz, Ejder: Medenî Usul Hukuku Ders Kitabı, 22.B., Ankara 2011, p. 215.

17 Gerçeker, Hasan: Anayasa Mahkemesine Bireysel Başvuru (Anayasa Şikayeti) Konulu Uluslararası Sempozyum Açılış Konuşması: "Bireysel Başvuru, Anayasa Şikayeti": HUKAB Sempozyum Serisi 1, 13 Mayıs 2011, p. 31;

Having noted that individual application is not a lawsuit in technical sense as mentioned above, we can say that this application mechanism is specific kind of lawsuit unique to constitutional law and that the term "lawsuit" is used in this sense[18]. However, it is neither necessary to use the concept of lawsuit nor is it appropriate to use the term "individual application lawsuit". The term "individual application" alone suffices to express the intended meaning without adding "lawsuit". Therefore, it is not appropriate to characterize the individual application mechanism as a type of lawsuit or to describe it with the concept of lawsuit.

Indeed, individual application is a complaint to the Constitutional Court due to violation of fundamental rights and freedoms by the public power. As a matter of fact, the concept of "constitutional complaint" is used in German law as mentioned above. There is a similar mechanism in our legal system. Pursuant to Article 16 and forthcoming articles of Enforcement and Bankruptcy Law one can lodge a complaint against the unlawful acts of the enforcement and bankruptcy directors. Although these ways are not exactly parallel to each other, both mechanism of application resemble to one another in terms of procedure and characteristics. The complaint is considered not to be a lawsuit in enforcement and bankruptcy law as well[19].

The legal nature of the individual application must also be examined within the context of appeal ways *(Rectsmittel)* – legal remedy *(Rechtsbehelf)*. This issue is of greater importance when we consider the provision of *"ordinary legal remedies must be exhausted"* in Article 148, paragraph III of the Constitution (Article 45, paragraph I of the CCL).

The distinction between way of appeal *(Rechtsmittel)* and legal remedy *(Rechtsbehelf)* exists in German law indeed. Way of appeal and legal remedy are the legally recognized means of legal protection for the protection of the benefits of the parties and the elimination of a disadvantage or an injurious consequence in the result of the decisions and acts of the judiciary organs[20]. When considered in this aspect, it is possible to accept the individual application mechanism as a legally recognized way or legal remedy for the elimination of the violations of individuals' fundamental rights and freedoms by the public power[21].

Besides, acting on this case, it should be recognized that the individual application bears the characteristics of a means of legal protection *(Rechtsschutzeinrichtung)* in general.

The "way of appeal" in the strict and technical sense has two characteristic effects: Contestation of the court's decision before a higher judicial organ and the prevention and delaying of the finalization of the decision in formal terms. Individual application does not bear these characteristics. For that reason, it is not possible to describe the individual application as a way of appeal in a strict and technical sense, as it does not meet these criteria[22]. Moreover, the purpose

---

Değnekli, Adnan: Yargıtay'ın Anayasa Şikayetine Bakışı: "Bireysel Başvuru, Anayasa Şikayeti", HUKAB Sempozyum Serisi 1, 13 Mayıs 2011, p. 81.

18   Örneğin bkz. Özbey p. 71.

19   Pekcanıtez, Hakan: İcra – İflâs Hukukunda Şikayet, Ankara 1986, p. 20 vd; Kuru, Baki / Arslan, Ramazan / Yılmaz, Ejder: İcra ve İflâs Hukuku Ders Kitabı, 24.B., Ankara 2010, p. 64. Tercan, Erdal /Tercan Süheyla: İcra ve İflâs Hukuku, Ankara 2005, p. 20.

20   Tercan, Erdal: Medeni Usul Hukukunda Kesin Sürelerin Kaçırılması Halinde Eski Hale Getirme, Ankara 2006, p. 56.

21   Ekinci, Hüseyin: Anayasa Mahkemesi Kanunu Çerçevesinde Bireysel Başvuruların İncelenme Usulü: "Bireysel Başvuru, Anayasa Şikayeti", HUKAB Sempozyum Serisi 1, 13 Mayıs 2011, p. 140.

22   Özbey p. 70.

and the scope of the way of appeal and the individual application are different from those of appeal ways in a strict and technical sense.

The legal remedies are divided into two as ordinary and extraordinary legal remedies. The legal remedies applied against decisions not finalized yet are ordinary legal remedies and those applied against the final decisions are called extraordinary legal remedies[23]. In this respect, as the individual application is a remedy that can be applied against the final court decisions, it can be described as an extraordinary legal remedy. It is also recognized in the doctrine to be a legal remedy of exceptional and subsidiary nature.[24]

C – Function and Purpose

There are certain fundamental rights and freedoms which constitute the basis of legal order, and such rights and freedoms must be observed by the state in a constitutional and democratic state of law. These rights and freedoms, which are the basic values of the state of law, constitute the cornerstones of the system and they can not be changed by the political will. Constitutional judiciary affords protection to these rights and freedoms in different forms. However, such protection remains to be limited without granting the individuals the right to individual application to the Constitutional Court. Practically, the constitutional order is protected to the best extent possible through initiating the way of exception or annulment actions. However, when compared to the protection through the application of the individuals directly to the Constitutional Court, such a protection remains to be indirect and limited.

Ensuring the recognition of the fundamental rights and freedoms as they are prescribed in the Constitution through granting the individuals the right to apply directly to the Constitutional Court, the individual application bears a vital importance with respect to the interpretation and improvement these rights in accordance with today's conditions. The individual application assumes an extremely important function with regards to the fact that individuals take an active role in the protection of the constitutional system and the realization of democratic participation as well as protecting their own rights and freedoms[25].

As it is explained in the previous part above, the primary purpose of the individual application is to ensure the protection of the fundamental rights and freedoms in the Constitution through the Constitutional Court when such rights and freedoms are not protected by other courts and ordinary legal remedies[26]. In addition to this subjective function of the individual application, it has an objective function to protect the legal order and to develop the constitutional law as well[27]. Moreover, it has a function to lead those exercising public power in the interpretation, execution and concretization of fundamental rights[28].

---

23 Kuru/Arslan/Yılmaz - Usul p. 600-601; Pekcanıtez/Atalay/Özekes p. 592.
24 Sabuncu, Yavuz / Arnwine Esen, Selin: Türkiye İçin Anayasa Şikayeti Model, Türkiye'de Bireysel Başvuru Yolu: Anayasa Yargısı, C.21, 2004, p. 236-242.
25 Mellinghof, Rudolf: Federal Almanya Cumhuriyetinde Anayasa Şikayeti: Anayasa Yargısı, C.26, 2009, p. 33.
26 Atasoy, p. 73; Sabuncu / Arnwine – Esen, p. 230.
27 Atasoy, p. 75.
28 Göztepe- Şikayet p. 17,20.

Taking the above mentioned functions of the individual application into consideration, we can say that it has four main functions[29] :
– To ensure the direct exercise and protection of rights and freedoms,
– To expand the scope of the constitutional interpretation principle,
– To ensure a unity in the judiciary with regards to the protection of fundamental rights and freedoms
– To contribute to the development of individuals' democratic awareness.
It must also be stated that another function attributed to the individual application in our country is to reduce the number of cases against Turkey before the ECtHR.

Taking these functions of the individual application into account, if we are to determine for what purposes the individual application mechanism has been adopted and whether the aimed purposes and the functions of the individual application overlap, we need to take a new look at the justifications for the amendment of Article 148 of the Constitution and Article 18 of the Law Nr. 5982 which introduced this remedy to our system. These justifications explain the aim of the adoption of the individual application as follows:

"… Numerous cases are filed against Turkey before the European Court of Human Rights each year and Turkey is sentenced to pay compensation in many cases. While examining the exhaustion of all domestic remedies, the European Court of Human Rights takes account of whether the individual application mechanism is implemented in the relevant country or not, and considers it to be an effective legal remedy in eliminating the violation of rights. Therefore, with the introduction of individual application mechanism, it is considered that a significant number of those alleging to be victim of violation of rights will be satisfied at individual application stage, namely before applying to the European Court of Human Rights, and that the number of cases to be filed and the decisions of violation to be rendered against Turkey will reduce. In this respect, establishment of a well-functioning individual application mechanism in Turkey will improve the standards on the basis of rights and the rule of law.…

The introduction of individual application mechanism in Turkey will ensure better protection of the fundamental rights and freedoms of individuals on one hand and force the public organs to abide by the Constitution and laws on the other hand. With the amendment made to that end, the citizens are entitled the right to individual application and Constitutional Court is assigned the duty to examine and rule on such applications for the protection and guaranteeing of individual rights and freedoms. …

The Constitutional Court has been attributed the mission to protect and extend the freedoms by means of reviewing the individual applications."[30]. The purposes mentioned here can be set under the following headings:
– To reduce the number of cases against Turkey before the ECtHR,
– To improve the standards on the basis of rights and the rule of law,
– To ensure better protection of the fundamental rights and freedoms of individuals,
– To force the public organs to abide by the Constitution and laws.

---

29 Sağlam; Fazıl: Anayasa Mahkemesinin 47. Kuruluş Yıldönümü Nedeniyle Düzenlenen "Bireysel Başvuru ve Dünyadaki Uygulaması" Konulu Sempozyum; Giriş ve Takdim Konuşması: Anayasa Yargısı 2009, Sayı 26, p. 27; Göztepe-Değerlendirme p. 21.
30 www: tbmm.gov.tr/sirasayi/dönem23/yıl01/ss497ek1, (date of accession: 04.08.2012).

In my opinion, except for the aim of reducing the number of cases against Turkey before the ECtHR, all other aims pursued befit the functions of the individual application. Indeed, it would be more appropriate not to mention the aim of reducing the number of cases against Turkey as one of the direct aims pursued. Because, this may be a requested result rather than an aim. To achieve this result, fundamental rights and freedoms must be protected and exercised; the standards must be improved on the basis of rights and the rule of law and the necessary sensitivity on the protection of the fundamental rights and freedoms must be created in the organs exercising public power, especially in other courts, in the first place. If the rights and freedoms of the individual are protected in this way and if they can exercise their rights as they are described in the Constitution, the number of cases filed against Turkey before the ECtHR will decrease automatically. Otherwise, if the rights and freedoms are not protected, the necessary diligence is not displayed; and the Constitutional Court cannot get through this workload, the individual application mechanism may be declared as an ineffective remedy by the ECtHR and, in this case, the number of the cases filed against Turkey will not decrease but may even increase in spite of the individual application mechanism and there will be a loss of prestige as well.

§.2 – Acts of public power which may be subject to individual application

A – In general terms

According to Article 148, paragraph 3 of our Constitution, one can resort to the individual application mechanism only if one of his/her fundamental rights and freedoms within the scope of the European Convention on Human Rights and which are guaranteed by the Constitution, has been violated by public power. Here the "public power" which causes the violation of the fundamental rights and freedoms should be clarified.

As it is known, there are three organs of the public power named in the Constitution which are legislative (Article 7), executive (8) and judiciary (9). Although one may think that individual application mechanism can be resorted against the acts of all these three organs, as it will be discussed in details below, Article 45, paragraph 3 of the CCL brings some significant limitations with the provision of *"Individual applications may not be lodged directly against legislative proceedings and regulatory administrative proceedings; proceedings excluded from judicial review by the Constitution and Constitutional Court judgments are not subject to individual application"*.

In terms of being subject to constitutional complaint, individual applications may be petitioned against the acts of all three organs in German law provided that the necessary conditions are satisfied[31].

The regulation is criticized in the doctrine[32] on the grounds that the notion of "public power" used in Article 148, paragraph 3 of the Constitution covers the legislative, executive and judiciary organs without any restriction; but the scope of public power is narrowed down with the regulation in Article 45, paragraph 3 of the CCL by leaving out the legislative proceedings and regulatory administrative proceedings

Another opinion on this issue is *"With reference to the "public power" used here, one should not assume that acts and proceedings of general and objective nature must also be considered in this context and that individual applications may be petitioned against them as well. Such an assumption will turn the individual application mechanism into abstract norm review. As a matter of fact, individual application is a mechanism adopted to review the violations of rights caused by the concrete application of the general norms. However, if the violation of right is caused by a general act or proceeding, such a general norm must be reviewed priorly by means of other judicial review mechanisms"*[33].

It can be claimed that the notion of "public power" used in Article 148, paragraph 3 of the Constitution covers the legislative, executive and judiciary organs and that regulatory administrative proceedings must also be subject to individual application. However, considering the aim of the adoption of the individual application mechanism, this limitation may have been

---

31   Mellinghof p. 36; Göztepe –Şikayet p. 42 vd.
32   Göztepe-Değerlendirme p. 27.
33   Sağlam –Bireysel Başvuru p. 48-49.

brought on such grounds as the probable workload that the Constitutional Court would confront with and the possibility that the individual application would turn into concrete norm review if individual applications could be petitioned against such administrative proceedings.

We will examine against which organs' acts and proceedings the individual application may be petitioned within the framework of these restrictions.

As Article 45, paragraph 2 of the CCL includes the phrase " *the proceeding, act or negligence which is alleged to have caused violation…* ", the proceeding or act of the public power alleged to have violated the rights or freedoms may be a negligence of an act or proceeding incumbent on the public power as well as an act or proceeding executed intentionally by the public power[34].

The act of the public power alleged to have violated the right or freedom must be executed within the geographical area under the sovereignty of the Republic of Turkey and by an organ of the Republic of Turkey. Individual application may not be petitioned against the acts or proceedings executed by the organs of a foreign state, or those of an international power.

As the individual application may be petitioned against the acts of the public power violating rights and freedoms, individual application cannot be lodged in principle against the interim acts or proceedings such as a survey conducted in a law case, an expert's opinion etc. which do not violate a right directly but serve as a preparation to a proceeding. For that reason, individual application must be petitioned only after the act or proceeding violating the right is finalized, e.g. the court must render its judgment and it must become final.

The internal acts and proceedings by and between the organs exercising public power which are not directly against the individuals, and are not of mandatory and binding nature for the individuals, e.g. a circulars, advisory decisions, advices etc., cannot be subject to individual application as they do not violate a right directly. As a matter of fact, the applicant does not have a legal interest in petitioning an individual application against such a proceeding.

In order to lodge an individual application, the proceeding alleged to have caused a violation must be executed by exercising public power and, thereby, bear a public law nature. As it is known, the organs exercising public power, especially the administration, does not necessarily act always by using the public power, but it may perform private law proceedings under certain conditions. When a lawsuit is to be filed against the administration with regards to the conflicts caused by such private law proceedings, the lawsuit must be petitioned to the judicial courts, not to the administrative courts. The reason is that the administration does not exercise a public power or does not force the individual to act in a certain manner in such cases. As there is a relation of equal interest between the parties, the parties engage in a legal relation with the administration in line with their interests and by their own will. In accordance with the basic logic in such cases, individual application may not be petitioned against the violations of rights caused by the private law proceedings of the administration.

---

34   Ekinci,Hüseyin /Sağlam, Musa: 66 Soruda Anayasa Mahkemesine Bireysel Başvuru, Ankara 2012, p. 13; Sabuncu/Arnwine-Esen p. 233.

B – Proceedings of the legislative organ

Article 148, paragraph 3 of the Constitution mentions the public power in general terms. It could be concluded that the proceedings of the legislative also fall within this scope and that individual application can be petitioned against the laws enacted. However, Article 45, paragraph 3 of the CCL states *"Individual applications may not be lodged directly against legislative proceedings and regulatory administrative proceedings"* and it is established that direct individual applications may not be petitioned against such proceedings[35]. The laws fall within the scope of the legislative proceedings in this clause and, in this context, budgetary laws of private nature, the law of final accounts, laws on the approval of the international treaties are also covered by this clause. Individual application cannot be petitioned against such proceedings. It must also be noted that international treaties should not be subject to individual application as well.

The Constitutional Court declares the applications against the provisions of the laws inadmissible on the grounds of *ratione materiae*[36].

---

[35] An annulment action was brought against this provision on the grounds that it is unconstiutional as it brings new restrictions which are not stipulated in Article 128 of the Constitution and this annulment action was dismissed with the decision nr. E.2011/59, K.201234 of the Constitutional Court dated 1.3.2013: *"The fact that individual applications may not be petitioned against legislative proceedings and regulatory administrative proceedings is related entirely to the nature of the right of individual application and such proceedings may not cause to the infringement of any individual right so long as they are not applied into practice. The legislative proceedings are subject to the review of the Constitutional Court through abstract and concrete norm reviewp. If their execution has led to violation of a right, the persons who suffered such a violation may apply to the Constiutional Court. Similarly, regulatory administrative proceedings are subject to direct review of the Council of State and if the execution of a regulatory administrative proceeding causes a violation of right, then the victim of such a violation may apply to the Constiutional Court as well.*

In other words, it is evident that the existence of a legislative proceeding or a regulatory administrative proceeding in the legal system *per se* may not principally cause a violation of right if it has not been implemented on the applicant in a concrete case. Therefore, individual applications may not be petitioned directly against such proceedings.

The fact that proceedings excluded from judicial review by the Constitution are not subject to individual application is a requirement of the Constitution. The legislative organ included such a regulation in the said rule subject to action entirely on the basis of the provisions of the Constitution on this matter.

The said rule which was brought before the Court also states that the Constitutional Court judgments may not be subject to individual application as well. Pursuant to the first paragraph of Article 149 of the Constiution, the Constitutional Court consists of two sections and the General Assembly. The second paragraph of the said Article states that the General Assembly shall hear the cases other than individual applications and the sections shall take the decision on individual applications. Paragraph nine of Article 148 and the first paraph of Article 153 of the Constiution states that the decisions of the Constitutional Court are final.

Considering the above mentioned provisions of the Constitution and Article 149 of the the Law on the Establishment and Rules of Procedure of the Constitutional Court, the legislative organ determined that decisions adopted by the General Assembly which are final under the Constitution provisions cannot be subject to a review to be conducted by the Sectionp. Therefore, the fact that no individual application may be petitioned against the decisions of the General Assembly which are final under the provisions of Article 148 and 153 of the Constitution cannot be considered as a limitation on the right to legal remediep."* http://www.anayasa.gov.tr/index.php?l= manage_k (date accessed: 22.07.2013)

[36] AYM 2.B. 2012/837, 5.3.2013: *"1. The applicant stated that he chaired the Executive Board of Batman Commodity Exchange Market for two successive term and that he cannot run as a candidate to a third term due to the provisions included in Article 40 of the Law on the Union Of Chambers And Commodity Exchanges Of Turkey and*

Is it possible to consider the decisions of the Parliament to fall within the scope of the legislative proceedings in this context? The proceedings of the Parliament in the form of a parliamentary decision which are different from laws in practice appear in various areas and they form a completely heterogeneous legal category[37]. The decisions of the Parliament are defined as the proceedings of the Turkish Grand National Assembly except laws. Yet another definition of the decisions of the parliament is "*The decisions adopted by the Turkish Grand National Assembly with regards to its internal structure and working order or the decisions adopted by the Turkish Grand National Assembly as part of its relations with the executive and judiciary organs*"[38]. If we are to express in general terms, as it is out of question for such decisions to violate individuals' rights, the decisions of the Parliament should also be exempted from individual application[39].

As the legislative proceedings are left out of the scope of the individual application, the negligence of the legislative organ, namely its failure to enact a certain law when it's obliged to do so, may not be subject to individual application in our law system[40].

C – Proceedings of the executive

All proceedings of the executive which is one of the three organs exercising public power are accepted as administrative proceedings in principle. To consider a certain proceeding to be of administrative nature, it does not matter which institution of the executive organ executed that proceeding[41]. Therefore, while examining whether the proceedings of the executive organ may be subject to individual application or not, it would be appropriate to carry out the examination considering the criteria for the administrative proceedings.

Although the proceedings of the executive are administrative proceedings in principle, some proceedings of the executive may be not administrative proceedings but private law pro-

---

Chambers and Commodity Exchanges Nr. 5174 dated 18/5/2004. The applicant alleged that the principle of equality and the right to vote and to be electedwhich are secured under the Constitution have been violated.

15. Individual application is a constitutional guarantee which determines the violation of fundamental rights suffered by the individuals and includes efficient tools for the elimination of such violationp. The individuals are not allowed under such guarantee to petition for the annulment legislative proceedingp.

16. The individual application mechanism to the Constitutional Court is not designed as a legal remedy which allows for alleging the unconstitutionality of an administrative proceeding in an abstract manner.

17. If a legislative proceeding causes the violation of a fundamental right or freedom, individual application may not be petitioned directly against the legislative proceeding itself but against the acts, proceedings or negligences which result from the execution of such legislative proceeding. In order to petition an individual application against such acts, proceedings or negligences, all legal remedies available must be exhausted in the first place.

18. It is alleged in the application petition that the third paragraph of Article 40 of the Law Nr. 5174 must be annulled on the grounds of unconstitutionality. Direct individual applications may not be petitioned to the Constiutional Court against legislative proceedings on the grounds of abstract unconstitutionality."

37 Teziç, Erdoğan: Parlamento Kararı ve Kanun: Anayasa Yargısı, C.5, 1989, p. 121.

38 Gözler Kemal: Türk Anayasa Hukuku Dersleri, 9.B, Bursa 2010, p. 244.

39 Sabuncu/Arnwine-Esen p. 233.

40 Although there is a principle in German law which includes an explicit constitututional provision allowing the individuals to demand a positive legislative proceeding subjectively, the negligence of the legislative organ may be mentioned if the necessary law is not enacted (Göztepe- şikayet p. 45).

41 Gözler, Kemal: İdare Hukuku Dersleri, 10. B., Bursa 2010, p. 270.

ceedings as it was mentioned above briefly. The fact that a proceeding is executed by the executive organ does not suffice to consider it as administrative proceeding; it must also be executed by exercising "public power". In this respect, individual application may be petitioned against the administrative proceedings executed by the executive organ by means of exercising public power. On the other hand, individual application may not be petitioned against the private law proceedings of by the executive organ. However, it should be noted that individual application may not be petitioned directly in the first instance against the administrative proceedings executed by the executive organ. If there are administrative or judicial remedies proposed against such proceedings, individual application may be petitioned only after the exhaustion of all those remedies and if the violation of a fundamental right has not been eliminated yet".

Administrative proceedings can be grouped in different aspects. This study will not elaborate on the types of administrative proceedings. However, we need to touch upon the types of administrative proceedings with regards to their being subject to individual application. The administrative proceedings are divided into two groups, one being unilateral and the other bilateral administrative proceedings[42]. The unilateral administrative proceedings are divided into two in itself: one being individual administrative proceedings and the other being regulatory administrative proceedings. Individual administrative proceedings are those specific to a certain individual or circumstance, e.g. the appointment of a public officer. The regulatory administrative proceedings, however, are not specific to a certain individual or circumstance and they bring a general and impersonal regulation such as bylaws or directives. As the Article 45, Paragraph 3 of the CCL includes the provision that direct individual applications may not be petitioned against regulatory administrative proceedings, we can conclude that such a distinction is predicated upon with regards to the administrative proceedings and whether they can be subject to individual application or not.

As the individual administrative proceedings are specific to a certain individual or circumstance, they may violate the individuals' rights and freedoms and, for that reason, individual applications may be petitioned against such proceedings. However, since the regulatory proceedings bring about a general and abstract regulation like the laws, they are not related to a specific person or circumstance. Therefore, it is out of question for such proceedings to directly violate the fundamental rights and freedoms of a specific person in principle. An individual proceeding should be made by the administration. For this reason, individual applications may not be petitioned against regulatory administrative proceedings. As a matter of fact, it is explicitly stated in Article 45, Paragraph 3 of the CCL that direct individual applications may not be lodged against regulatory administrative proceedings.

D – Proceedings of the judiciary organs

Individual applications may be petitioned against proceedings of the judiciary as it is another organ exercising public power. In fact, all the provisions both in the Constitution and the CCL relating to the individual application create an impression that individual application mecha-

---

42   Gözler – İdare p. 274 vd.

nism is regulated so as to address against the court decisions. As a matter of fact, as it is examined above within the framework of the current regulation, individual applications may not be petitioned against legislative proceedings and regulatory administrative proceedings. The individual administrative proceedings of the executive organ may be subject to individual application. However, before petitioning such an application, all administrative and judicial remedies proposed in our law must be exhausted, a lawsuit must be filed and all ways of appeal such as objection, appeal, cassation or such other remedies available against the court decision must also be exhausted(Article 45, Paragraph 2 of the CCL). In this case, individual application is petitioned similarly against the court decision. Individual application can be petitioned against the decision of the criminal or civil courts as well. Similarly, all ways of appeal such as objection, appeal, cassation or such other remedies available against the decisions of the courts of instances must also be exhausted. In its current status in our law, the individual application seems to be a remedy available largely against the court decisions.

As it is known, the court decisions may be either final or interim decisions. In principle, individual application may be petitioned only against the final decisions of the courts. These decisions may be related to the acceptance or dismissal on merits of the case or they may be decisions of dismissal on the grounds of form. As it was stated before, all legal remedies available against that court decision must be exhausted before petitioning an individual application against the final decision of the courts.

In principle, individual applications may not be petitioned against the interim court decisions. However, as a matter of course, it is an exigency to resort to the individual application mechanism against certain exceptional interim court decisions.

In terms of our law, there is no explicit provision which prescribes that individual applications may not be petitioned against the interim decisions. However, as it was explained above, we can conclude from the regulations that individual applications may only be petitioned against the final decisions of the courts in principle. Nevertheless, it is possible to accept individual applications against certain interim decisions of the courts through the case-law of the Constitutional Court. Especially, if a decision authorizing a detention is challenged (Article 101, Paragraph 5 the Penal Procedure Law (PPL)) and such challenge is dismissed, it should be available to petition an individual application against such a decisions of dismissal[43]. According to Article 108, Paragraph 1 of the PPL, the detention must be reviewed in every thirty-day periods or, as per paragraph three, in every hearing or hearing recess when the circumstances demand so. In such a circumstance, individual application should not be petitioned against every decision for continued detention. Otherwise, it would be required to petition an individual application against detention decisions given once in very thirty-day period or the decisions on continuation of detention given in each hearing. The workload of the Constitutional Court would unbearably increase. In my opinion, if there has been a significant change in the grounds for detention, or the detention period has become too long in consideration of the offence alleged, individual application must be available in that case against the dismissal of the

---

43   See for example AYM 2.Bl., Application Nr: 2012/521, Decision Date: 2.7.2013: http://www.anayasa.gov.tr/
index. php?l= manage_k (date of accession: 22.07.2013).

request for release. The case-law of Constitutional Court to be established in time will shape the decisions on such applications.

In trial proceedings exceeding the reasonable time period, it is not required to wait until the finalization of the case. As a matter of fact, the Court agreed that the reasonable time period for trial has been exceeded in a cadastre case which had lasted for longer than 10 years and ruled for violation without waiting the conclusion of the case[44].

According to Article 45, Paragraph 3 of the CCL, the Constitutional Court judgments[45] and proceedings excluded from judicial review by the Constitution are not subject to individual application.

---

44 AYM 1.Bl., Application Nr: 2012/13, Decision Date: 2.7.2013: http://www.anayasa.gov.tr/index.php?l= manage_k (date of accession: 22.07.2013).

45 Pursuant to Article 3 of the CCL, the duties and powers of the Constitutional Court are as follows:
"a) To deal with annulment cases filed on the grounds that laws, decree-laws and the Internal Regulation of the Grand National Assembly of Turkey or certain articles or provisions thereof are alleged to be against the Constitution as to the form and merits, and that constitutional amendments alleged to be contradicting with the Constitution in terms of their form.
b) To conclude contested matters referred by courts to the Constitutional Court pursuant to Article 152 of the Constitution.
c) To conclude individual applications filed pursuant to Article 148 of the Constitution.
ç) To try, in its capacity as the Grand Court, the President of the Republic, Speaker of the Grand National Assembly of Turkey, members of the Council of Ministers; the presidents, members of the Constitutional Court, the Court of Cassation, the Council of State, the Military Court of Cassation, the Military Supreme Administrative Court, chief public prosecutors, deputy chief public prosecutors, the president and members of the High Council of Judges and Prosecutors and the Court of Accounts, the Chief of General Staff, Chiefs of Land, Naval and Air Forces and Gendarmerie General Commander due to offenses relating to their dutiep.
d) To conclude cases concerning dissolution of political parties and their deprivation of state aid, warning applications and requests for determination of the status of dissolution.
e) To audit or to have audited lawfulness of property acquisitions by political parties and their revenues and expenditurep.
f) In case the Grand National Assembly of Turkey resolves to remove parliamentary immunity or revoke membership of the parliamentary deputies or remove the immunity of the non-deputy ministers, to conclude annulment requests of the concerned or other deputies alleging repugnance (of relevant resolution) to the provisions of the Constitution, law or the Internal Regulation of the Grand National Assembly of Turkey.
g) To elect the President and deputy presidents of the Constitutional Court and the President and deputy president of the Court of Disputes amongst members of the Court.
ğ) To carry out other duties set forth in the Constitution."

§.3 – Determining the rights and freedoms which may be subject to individual application

A – In general terms

There are two provisions regarding the determination of rights which may be subject to individual application: one is Article 148, Paragraph 3 of the Constitution and the other is Article 45 of the CCL. Article 148, Paragraph 3 of the Constitution reads as "*Everyone may apply to the Constitutional Court on the grounds that one of the fundamental rights and freedoms within the scope of the European Convention on Human Rights which are guaranteed by the Constitution has been violated by public authorities*". The provision refers both to the Constitution and the European Convention on Human Rights (ECHR) for the determining of the rights which may be subject to individual application.

Similarly, Article 45, Paragraph 1 of the CCL reads as "*Every person may apply to the Constitutional Court alleging that the public power has violated any one of his/her fundamental rights and freedoms secured under the Constitution which falls into the scope of the European Convention on Human Rights and additional protocols thereto, which Turkey is a party to.*" Article 148, Paragraph 3 of the Constitution and the said provision are parallel to each other. However, an additional phrase of "*and additional protocols thereto, to which Turkey is a party .*" is added to Article 45, Paragraph 1 of the CCL and, thereby, the additional protocols of the ECHR are also included among the texts to be referred to in determining the rights which may be subject to individual application.

Making regulations referring to the ECHR in determining the rights which may be subject to individual application is not a new case which came up for the first time with the Constitutional amendments in 2010. Previously, a similar method was used in the constitution proposals prepared in the past[46] and even in the Constitutional amendment proposal prepared by the Constitutional Court itself[47].

Within the framework of Article 148, Paragraph 3 of the Constitution and Article 45, Paragraph 1 of the CCL, in order to determine the rights which may be subject to individual application, we need to look into both the fundamental rights and freedoms cited in the Constitution and the ECHR and the additional protocols to which Turkey is a party. However, it must be stated as a preliminary assessment that the rights which may be subject to individual application are essentially the fundamental rights and freedoms secured under the Constitution. It can be said that the phrase "the European Convention on Human Rights and additional protocols thereto, to which Turkey is a party" is intended to define the scope[48], better to say to

---

46 For instance, proposals dated 2001 and 2007 prepared by Turkish Union of Chambers and Exchange Commodities.

47 Tülen, Hikmet: Anayasa Mahkemesinin Yeniden Yapılandırılmasına İlişkin Anayasa Değişikliği Taslağı Üzerine Açıklamalar ve Birkaç Öneri, http://www.e-akademi.org/makaleler/htulen-1.htm (date of accession: 16.07.2013).

48 Göztepe-Değerlendirme p. 35.

limit the scope[49]. As a consequence of this, certain rights and freedoms which are secured under the Constitution but do not fall into the scope of the European Convention on Human Rights and additional protocols to which Turkey is a party, will inevitably be left out of the scope and will not be subject to individual application. For instance, such rights as freedom to work and conclude contracts in Article 48, the right and duty to work in Article 49, working conditions and right to rest and leisure in Article 50 and the right to enter public service in Article 70 of the Constitution may be cited among these rights.

With this formula used to determine the rights which may be subject to individual application, the references made in the Constitution to the ECHR and the reference made in Article 45, Paragraph 1 of the CCL to additional protocols to which Turkey is a party have caused to emergence of various different opinions. According to an opinion[50], as the rights which may be subject to individual application are not the rights included in the ECHR and its additional protocols but those corresponding to such rights in the Constitution, if a right included in one of the additional protocols is violated and if there is a right corresponding to it in the Constitution, then that right must be subject to individual application regardless of whether Turkey is a party to that protocol or not. Because the language of the text is preferred to leave out the rights formulated as "State responsibilities" which are already excluded from the regular scope of implementation of the individual application.

Indeed, the phrase "*and additional protocols thereto, to which Turkey is a party*" brought with Article 45, Paragraph 1 of the CCL causes an absurd restriction in the list of the rights which may be subject to individual application and this situation is expressly against the purpose and scope of the formula in the Constitution. According to this opinion again, while determining the effect and the scope of the rights and freedoms which may be subject to individual application, the guarantees in our Constitution which broaden the effect and the scope of the rights and freedoms must also be included within the scope of the individual application even if they are not covered in the ECHR

According to another opinion proposed[51], Article 148, Paragraph 3 of the Constitution and Article 45, Paragraph 1 of the CCL must be interpreted together. In order for a fundamental right or a freedom to be subject to an individual application, it is not enough to be secured under the Constitution but it must also be included in either the ECHR or one of the additional protocols thereto, which Turkey is a party to. If a right is secured under the Constitution but not covered in the ECHR or its additional protocols to which Turkey is a party, such a right may not be subject to individual application. Therefore, the rights regulated in the additional protocols may not be subject to individual application even if they are secured under the Constitution. As a result of this, as Turkey is not a party to Protocols Nr. 4, 7 and 12, the rights and freedoms[52] covered in these Protocols may not be subject to individual application. While

---

49   Göztepe-Değerlendirme p. 35.

50   Sağlam, Fazıl: Anayasa Şikayeti Anlamı, Kapsamı ve Türkiye Uygulamasında Olası Sorunlar: Demokratik Anayasa (Görüşler Öneriler), Editör: Aykut Çelebi, Ece Göztepe, Ankara 2011, p. 430-431.

51   Doğru, Osman: Anayasa İle Karşılaştırmalı İnsan Hakları Avrupa Sözleşmesi ve Mahkeme İçtüzüğü, İstanbul 2010, p. 5; Çoban 165.

52   Article 1 of Protocl Nr. 4, that no one shall be deprived of his liberty merely on the ground of inability to fulfil a contractual obligation. (Article 38,8 of the Constitution); Article 2, freedom of residence and movement (Article 23 of the Constitution); Article 5 of Protocl Nr. 7, equality between spouses (Article 41,7 of the Constitution).

determining the effect and scope of the rights and freedoms which may be subject to individual application, the fact that a right is designated both in the Constitution and the ECHR under the same name is not sufficient by itself to consider that right within the scope of the individual application. It must also be examined whether there is equivalence between the Constitution and the ECHR with regards to the scope of a right[53].

Within the framework of Article 148, Paragraph 3 of the Constitution and Article 45, Paragraph 1 of the CCL, in order to determine the rights which may be subject to individual application, we need to look into both the fundamental rights and freedoms cited in the Constitution and the ECHR and the protocols to which Turkey is a party. It is important to note on this issue that the Constitution and the ECHR and its additional protocols are not alternative to one another but they are cumulative, i.e. for a fundamental right or freedom to be subject to individual application, it must be included both in the Constitution and in the ECHR or its additional protocols. The rights and freedoms may not be subject to individual application if they are secured under the Constitution alone or if they are covered only in the ECHR or the additional protocols thereto, to which Turkey is a party. They must be regulated in both to be subject to individual application.

In this context, it must also be noted that a fundamental right or freedom secured under the Constitution does not have to be included both in the ECHR and in its additional protocols which Turkey is a party. In this sense, the ECHR and the Protocols are alternative to one another and it is sufficient if the said right is regulated in either one of them.

The fact that the rights which may be subject to individual application are regulated by making reference to the Constitution and the ECHR and the Protocols ratified by Turkey brings about many concerns in determining which rights or freedoms may be subject to application and defining the scope of such rights and freedoms.

The rights which may be subject to individual application could be regulated directly within the scope of the fundamental rights and freedoms stated in the Constitution without making any reference to the ECHR. Similarly, reference could be made to the relevant articles of the Constitution and the rights aimed to be covered within the scope of application could be cited while leaving the remaining right and freedoms out of scope. Such a method could have been more practical. As a matter of fact, the rights which may be subject to individual application were identified on the basis of the Constitution in such countries as German and Spain, where the individual application (constitutional complaint) is applied. When the fundamental rights and freedoms secured under the Constitution are taken as basis, it must also be noted that most of the regulations in the Constitution are more comprehensive than those in the ECHR. By making reference to the ECHR and the protocols which Turkey is a party to, the legislative organ aimed to reduce the number violation decisions given against Turkey as explained above and it also aimed to prevent a drastic increase in the workload of the Constitutional Court by imposing a second limitation on the rights which may be subject to individual application.

Restricting the rights which may be subject to individual application by making reference to the ECHR and the protocols to which Turkey is a party, may contribute to reducing the workload

---

53   Sağlam - Haklar p. 271;Çoban p. 165.

of the Constitutional Court in statistical terms. However, as it will be discussed in details below, this formula will bring about many uncertainties in determining the rights which may be subject to individual application and the scope of such rights and, therefore, will cause an additional workload to the Constitutional Court. The Constitutional Court will struggle to eliminate such uncertainties through its case-law which may take years. Moreover, the fact that not all protocols of the ECHR but only those ratified by Turkey contradicts with the aim *"to improve the standards on the basis of rights and the rule of law"* which is cited among the grounds for the adoption of individual application mechanism.

Making reference to the ECHR and its additional protocols in determining the rights which may be subject to individual application aims to limit the scope with the classic rights only and leave the social and economic rights out of the scope. On the other hand, taking the difficulty in separating the social and economic rights from classic rights under certain circumstances into consideration, the ECHR is called out to narrow down the list of rights. If the social and economic rights are recognized among the ones which may be subject to individual application, this will bring along many problems indeed. Because, the exercise of such rights is subject to a positive action of the State and includes program provisions. If the Court enters into this field and conducts a review, this may result in the Court's intervention to the economic and social policies of the government: This would pose a risk to shift to a review of expediency and confront the Court with an unbearable workload[54].

B – Rights and freedoms subject to individual application

As it is mentioned above, the rights and freedoms which may be subject to individual application are regulated in our law by making reference to the Constitution and the ECHR within the framework of Article 148, Paragraph 3 of the Constitution and Article 45, Paragraph 1 of the CCL. In consideration of this condition, in order to determine whether a right may be subject to individual application or not, we need to look into both the Constitution and the ECHR and the protocols which Turkey is a party to. Although a reference is made to the ECHR and its additional protocols, it must be noted in the first place that the rights which may be subject to individual application are essentially the fundamental rights and freedoms secured under the Constitution. As a matter of fact, this is explicitly emphasized both in Article 148, Paragraph 3 of the Constitution and Article 45, Paragraph 1 of the CCL with the phrase of *"… one of the fundamental rights and freedoms …which are guaranteed by the Constitution…"* However, a fundamental right or freedom guaranteed by the Constitution cannot be subject to individual application directly. In order for that right to be subject to individual application, it must also be included in either the ECHR or additional protocols thereto, to which Turkey is a party, i.e. such a right must be regulated in both the Constitution and the ECHR or its protocols and there must be convergence of these two. Article 45, Paragraph 1 of the CCL expresses this as *"… which falls into the scope of the European Convention on Human Rights and additional protocols thereto, to which Turkey is a party…"* Although the text of the law links the ECHR and the pro-

---

54   Sağlam – Haklar p. 275.

tocols with the conjunction word "*and*" and makes out a meaning as if a right or freedom must be included both in the ECHR and the protocols thereto, to which Turkey is a party, this conjunction word must be interpreted as "*or*" and the scope must be determined accordingly. Therefore, the said phrase must be interpreted as "*...which falls into the scope of the European Convention on Human Rights **or** additional protocols thereto, to which Turkey is a party...*" Because, as it is known, a right or freedom is not regulated both in the ECHR and its additional protocols separately. It is regulated either in the main text of the Convention or in its additional protocols.

It must also be noted that it is quite difficult to establish congruence between the fundamental rights and freedoms secured under our Constitution and the rights and freedoms which fall into the scope of the ECHR and additional protocols thereto, to which Turkey is a party, both in terms of their denomination and their scopes. The Constitutional Court will build up a list of rights and freedoms which may be subject to individual application through the Court's case-law to be created in the course time. In this context, the Constitutional Court is obliged to consider not only the texts and wording of the ECHR and its additional protocols but also the decisions of ECtHR, which is recognized to be a living judicial system[55]. When we consider the extensive interpretation of rights by the judgments of ECtHR and which relate the fundamental rights regulated in the ECHR and its protocols to the social rights, thereby, including the social rights into the scope protection, this point becomes extremely important.

Various lists of rights which may be subject to individual application have been prepared by overlapping the rights secured under our Constitution and those covered in the ECHR and additional protocols thereto, to which Turkey is a party[56]. While preparing those lists, it seems that the rights covered in the ECHR and additional protocols thereto, have been taken as basis and the corresponding rights secured under our Constitution are stated. In conclusion, although the rights secured under the Constitution are broader, all the constitutional rights other than those enumerated in the ECHR and its additional protocols may not be subject to individual application. However, in spite of this occasion, it would be appropriate to take the rights secured under Constitution as basis and determine the rights which may be subject to individual application accordingly. The rights and freedoms which may be subject to individual application can be listed as follows:

Constitution	the ECHR and Protocols Ratified
ARTICLE 17: Personal Inviolability, Corporal and Spiritual Existence of the Individual	ARTICLE 2 – Right to Life ARTICLE 3 – Prohibition of Torture
ARTICLE 18: Prohibition of Forced Labour	ARTICLE 4 – Prohibition of Slavery and Forced Labour

---

55 Göztepe – Değerlendirme p. 37.

56 Bkz. Sabuncu/Arnwine - Esen, p. 236-242; Göztepe –Değerlendirme p. 35; Görgün, Emin /Aydın, Yakup: Sayıştay Kararlarına Karşı Anayasa Mahkemesine Bireysel Başvuru Yolu: Sayıştay Dergisi, Yıl 2012, Sayı:84, p. 70-71.

Constitution	the ECHR and Protocols Ratified
ARTICLE 19: Personal Liberty and Security, Privacy and Protection of Private Life	ARTICLE 5 – Right to Liberty and Security
ARTICLE 20: Privacy of Private Life	ARTICLE 8 : Right to respect for private and family life
ARTICLE 21: Inviolability of the Domicile	ARTICLE 8 : Right to respect for private and family life
ARTICLE 22: Freedom of Communication	ARTICLE 8 : Right to respect for private and family life
ARTICLE 23: Freedom of Residence and Movement	–
ARTICLE 24: Freedom of Religion and Conscience	ARTICLE 9 : Freedom of thought, conscience and religion
ARTICLE 25: Freedom of Thought and Opinion	ARTICLE 9 : Freedom of thought, conscience and religion
ARTICLE 26: Freedom of Expression a nd Dissemination of Thought	ARTICLE 9 : Freedom of thought, conscience and religion, ARTICLE 10: Freedom of expression
ARTICLE 27: Freedom of Science and the Arts, Provisions relating to the Press and Publication	ARTICLE 9 : Freedom of thought, conscience and religion, ARTICLE 10: Freedom of expression
ARTICLE 28: Freedom of the Press	ARTICLE 9 : Freedom of thought, conscience and religion, ARTICLE 10: Freedom of expression
ARTICLE 29: Right to Publish Periodicals and Non-periodicals	ARTICLE 9 : Freedom of thought, conscience and religion, ARTICLE 10: Freedom of expression
ARTICLE 30: Protection of Printing Facilities	ARTICLE 9 : Freedom of thought, conscience and religion, ARTICLE 10: Freedom of expression
ARTICLE 31: Right to use Media other than the Press Owned by Public Corporations	ARTICLE 9 : Freedom of thought, conscience and religion, ARTICLE 10: Freedom of expression
ARTICLE 32: Right of Rectification and Reply, Rights and Freedoms of Assembly	ARTICLE 9 : Freedom of thought, conscience and religion, ARTICLE 10: Freedom of expression
ARTICLE 33: Freedom of Association	ARTICLE 11: Freedom of assembly and association

Constitution	the ECHR and Protocols Ratified
ARTICLE 34: Right to hold Meetings and Demonstration Marches	ARTICLE 11: Freedom of assembly and association
ARTICLE 35: Right to Property	ADDITIONAL PROTOCOL 1., ARTICLE 1: Protection of property
ARTICLE 36: Freedom to claim Rights	ARTICLE 6 : Right to a fair trial ARTICLE 13: Right to an effective remedy
ARTICLE 37: Principle of Natural Judge	ARTICLE 6 : Right to a fair trial
ARTICLE 38: Principles relating to Offences and Penalties	ARTICLE 6 : Right to a fair trial
ARTICLE 39: Right to prove an Allegation	ARTICLE 6 : Right to a fair trial
ARTICLE 40: Protection of Fundamental Rights and Freedoms	ARTICLE 6 : Right to a fair trial ARTICLE 13: Right to an effective remedy

Additionally:
- Right of education regulated under Article 42 of the Constitution matches up to the Right of education regulated under Article 2 of the 1st Additional Protocol;
- Right to vote and to be elected regulated under Article 67 of the Constitution matches up to the right to participate in free elections regulated under Article 3 of the 1st Additional Protocol. The Constitutional Court may consider these rights within the scope of the individual application through the Court's case-law.

Accordingly, the rights and freedoms which may not be subject to individual application as they are secured under the Constitution but not included in the ECHR or included in the additional Protocols 4, 7 and 12, to which Turkey is not a party, can be defined as follows[57]:
- Protocol 4 Art. 1 – Prohibition of deprivation of liberty on the ground of inability to fulfill a contractual obligation – Constitution Art. 38/8,
- Protocol 4 Art. 2 – Freedom of movement – Constitution Art. 23,
- Protocol 4 Art. 3 – Prohibition of expulsion of nationals – Constitution Art.23/6,
- Protocol 4 Art. 4 – Prohibition of collective expulsion of aliens – Constitution Art. 16,
- Protocol 7 Art. 2 – Right of appeal in criminal matters – Constitution Art. 36/1,
- Protocol 7 Art. 3 – Right of compensation for erroneous conviction – Constitution Art. 40/3; m. 19/9,
- Protocol 7 Art. 4 – Right not to be tried or punished twice – Constitution Art. 36/1; 38,
- Protocol 7 Art. 5 – Equality between spouses - Constitution Art.41/1,
- Protocol 12 Art. 1 (general prohibition of discrimination) – Constitution Art. 10, (however, Art.10 of the Constitution may be considered within the scope of Article 14 of the ECHR). Although Article 10 of the Constitution regulates the principle of equality in general, it may possibly not be subject to individual application on its own as a principle

---

57 Göztepe – Değerlendirme p. 36.

which secures the equality in exercise of a certain right or freedom. The principle of equality in general terms could be subject to individual application on its own if it is recognized as an independent fundamental right. However, the Constitutional Court did not recognize the principle of equality as an independent right in its decisions but held that individual application could be petitioned against the violation of the principle of equality in exercise of another fundamental right or freedom.

It is stated in the doctrine[58] that, with reference to the ECHR and additional protocols, such rights as right to life, prohibition of torture or ill-treatment, prohibition of slavery and forced labor, right to liberty and security, right to a fair trial, principle of no punishment without law, right to respect for private and family life, freedom of thought, conscience and religion, freedom of expression, freedom of assembly and association, right to marry, right to an effective remedy, prohibition of discrimination, right to property, right to education and right to free elections may be subject to individual application.

As it is shown comparatively in the table above, the fundamental rights and freedoms under Article 17 to Article 40 of our Constitution, excluding those regulated under Additional Protocols 4, 7 and 12 of the ECHR, to which Turkey is not a party, may be subject to individual application. Furthermore, "the right to education" regulated under Article 42 in Chapter "Social and Economic Rights and Duties" of the Constitution and "the right to vote, to be elected and to engage in political" regulated under Article 67 in Chapter "Political Rights and Duties" of the Constitution should also be recognized among the fundamental rights which may be subject to individual application as they are regulated in Additional Protocol 1(Art. 2, 3) to which Turkey is a party[59].

It should be noted that although these rights, defined by name, which may be subject to individual application, the Constitutional Court will determine the context and scope of application for these rights.

---

58 Doğru – Bireysel Başvuru p. 5 vd.; Sağlam – Haklar p. 291 vd.; Ekinci/Sağlam p. 12-13.
59 These rights and freedoms which are recognized to be subject to individual application are not further examined here.

§.4 – Determining the persons entitled to individual application

A – In general

With regards to the persons who may lodge individual application, Article 148 of the Constitution and Article 45,Paragraph 1 of the CCL uses the phrase "everyone". However, it is not further explained who are meant with the word of "everyone". Article 46, Paragraph 1 of the CCL titled "Persons entitled to individual application" defines in general terms who are entitled to individual application in principle by stating *"Individual applications may only be filed by those whose actual and personal rights are directly affected by the alleged proceeding, act or negligence which has caused the violation"* . As it is seen in this provision which we can accept as a general rule regarding the persons entitled to individual application, no specific persons or groups are cited in accordance with "everyone" phrase but it is recognized that anyone whose fundamental right is effected by the public power may petition an individual application by stating "those whose rights are directly affected". However, the second and third paragraphs of Article 46 of the CCL bring certain exemptions to this general principle and a restriction is imposed by citing who may not petition an application, or in which context and scope the application may be petitioned. The mentioned provisions are as follows:

"(2) Public legal persons may not petition individual applications. Private-law legal persons may apply solely on the grounds that their rights concerning legal personality have been violated.

(3) Foreigners may not petition individual applications concerning rights exclusive to Turkish citizens."

It is evident that the phrase "everyone" in the Constitution and the relevant law is used in the first place to mean the parties to the proceeding or act of the public power and, in case of lawsuit, the parties of the lawsuit. However, as the third persons may be a party to the lawsuit under certain circumstances and their rights may be affected as well, such third persons are also included within the meaning of "everyone" phrase.

B – The status of the real persons and legal persons

We will analyze the status of the real persons and legal persons with regards to their entitlement to lodge individual application under this title. The required qualifications sought in those to petition an individual application must be established in the first place. The relation between the applicant and the public power violating the right, i.e. being affected by the alleged proceeding, as a requirement of entitlement to individual application will not be mentioned here but this issue will be analyzed below separately[60]. The applicant must in the first place have legal capacity to be a party and the legal capacity to lodge individual application. Now, we will

---

60   See. aşa. §.5, B,II et al.

analyze the legal capacity to be a party and the legal capacity to lodge an individual individual application in details with regards to the real persons and legal persons.

I – Legal Capacity to be a Party

The capacity is a personal *sine qua non* to petition an application or to be the applicant or complaining party. The legal capacity to be a party in an individual application is, in principle, a manifestation or extension of the *capacity of using rights* in civil law. Therefore, persons who have the *capacity of using rights* in civil law also have the legal capacity to petition individual application in principle. As the real persons (Art. 8 of the Civil Code) and legal persons (Art. 48 of the Civil Code) have the *capacity of using rights* in civil law, they also have the capacity to petition individual application in principle. However, the capacity of real persons and legal persons with regards to individual application has certain features and it would help to give them a closer look an analysis.

1 – Real Persons

Article 8, Paragraph 1 of the Turkish Civil Code states "*Every person is entitled to a vested right*" Similarly, according to Article 28, "*Personality begins at the very moment the child is full born and ends by death. – The child possesses the right of capacity at the very moment he/she enters mother's womb provided that he/she is born alive.*" Therefore, every real person possesses the right of capacity, and hence the legal capacity to be a party with regards to the individual application, at the very moment he/she enters mother's womb provided that he/she is born alive. Such capacity continues for the whole life and ends with the death of person in principle.

As the beneficiaries of the fundamental rights and freedoms secured under the Constitution, the real persons' being a party to the individual application and their claim before the Constitutional Court through individual application for their rights and freedoms alleged to have been violated constitutes the main duty field of the individual application. Fundamental rights and freedoms ensure that a person is born as an individual, leads a life that benefits human dignity, improves his/her material and spiritual wellbeing and that certain fields of freedom are created. These rights and freedoms also secure that the individual participates in, creates an effect on and benefits from the social life. Accordingly, all real persons affected by the Turkish public power have the contractual capacity to petition an individual application. In this context, the foreigner may also petition individual application for certain rights[61].

The fetus possesses the legal capacity to own rights at the very moment he/she enters mother's womb provided that he/she is born alive. If the benefits of the fetus require so, the custodian of the child may appoint an administrative guardian (TCC Art. 427/3).

The right of capacity, and hence the legal capacity to be a party, of the real persons ends with their death (TCC Artc. 28, Paragraph 1). Therefore a dead person may not be a party to the individual application. Under these circumstances, individual application may not be petitioned in principle on behalf of a person for the protection of that person's fundamental rights and freedoms if the said person had died before the date of application.

If the applicant dies after the petitioning of the individual application, in that case, the legal capacity of the applicant to be a party ends, too. It is not possible in principle to continue the

---

61   The status of the foreigners will be examined below separately, see. §. 4,C.

application proceedings on his behalf after his death. However, it can not be said the filed application ends immediately after the death of the applicant. The solution method[62] implemented in civil lawsuits in case of the plaintiff's death during the case proceedings may also be implemented here to determine on the consequence by making a comparison between the circumstances. Accordingly, a distinction must be made with regards to whether the application will expire with the death of the applicant or not. If the subject matter of the application is related to only the applicant himself and does not pass on to his heirs (e.g. applications relating to immaterial rights), in that case the application becomes devoid of essence and must be dismissed. On the other hand, if the subject matter of the application is related not only to the applicant himself but also to his heirs (e.g. applications relating to property rights), the application does not become devoid of essence. In that case, the lawsuit must be followed and maintained by the heirs of the application all together. Article 55 of the Code of Civil Procedure may be implemented for such a case by analogy.

2 – Legal Persons

Legal persons also have the capacity of having rights and the legal capacity to be a party in a law-suit accordingly. As it is known, legal persons are divided into two: one is the public legal persons and the other is private law legal persons. Article 46, Paragraph 2 of the CCL regulates the status of the public legal persons and private law legal persons with regards to the individual application separately. For that reason, it would be appropriate to analyze their entitlement to individual application separately.

a – Private Law Legal Persons

Private Law Legal Persons are companies of persons or assets having legal personalities which are established under the private law and do not represent the public authority. Some examples of such legal persons are associations, foundations, and commercial companies. By attaining legal personality in due form, such legal persons also become the possessor of the capacity of using rights. Article 48 of the Turkish Civil Code states "*The legal entities are entitled to use all the rights vested upon and the capacity to undertake all kinds of obligations other than the characteristics related to real persons such as sex, age, kinship etc.*" As it is seen, the legal persons possess all the rights and freedoms except for the fundamental rights and freedoms characteristically specific to human. Therefore, they have the right of capacity with regards to the individual application. When viewed from this aspect, the legal persons may be entitled to many rights and freedoms secured under the Constitution. Some of the examples to such rights are equality before law (Art. 10), personal inviolability (Art. 17), freedom of communication (Art. 22), right to property (Art. 35), freedom to claim rights, right to a fair trial (Art. 36), principal of natural judge (Article 37) etc.

With the termination legal personality, the right of capacity, and hence the legal capacity to be a party, of the legal person ends. From then on, the legal person may not be a party to an individual application on its own behalf. Upon the termination of the legal personality, the property of that legal person will be inherited to the legal person who is legal successor. If the subject matter of the individual application is related to property, the legal person successor to the rights should be entitled to continue the individual application proceedings. If the indi-

---

62   See, Kuru /Arslan /Yılmaz – Usul, p. 221 vd.

vidual application is not related to property, the application should become devoid of essence with the termination of the legal personality.

Article 46, Paragraph 2 of the CCL includes the provision of "…*Private-law legal persons may apply solely on the grounds that their rights concerning legal personality have been violated*". Accordingly, the private law legal persons may not petition individual application; but may apply solely on the grounds that their rights concerning legal personality have been violated. For example, an association may petition an individual application if its own property right is violated but may not file an application against a public power proceeding relating to the rights and benefits of its members[63]. Similarly, an association for the protection of consumer rights may not petition an individual application for the protection of consumers even if there is a relevant provision in the statue of the association; it can file individual application only against the public power proceedings relating to its legal personality.

As it is seen, the legislative organ has narrowed down the scope of individual application with regards to the private law legal persons by enacting the said provision. It can be said that one of the concerns for this limitation is to keep the workload of the Constitutional Court at a reasonable and bearable level.

b – Public Legal Persons

Public legal persons shall be established only by law, or by the authority expressly granted by law (Art. 123 of the Constitution). Public legal persons, as a requirement of their duties, exercise public power and represent the public authority. The state has public legal personality and the ministries are the organs of the state public personality. In addition to the state, general directorates of the ministries, special provincial administrations, municipalities, villages, public economic enterprises and their affiliated institutions have public legal personalities.

In principle, public legal persons also have legal capacity to be a party, and they could have the legal capacity with regards to the individual application. However, Article 46, Paragraph 2 of the CCL explicitly includes the provision of "*Public legal persons may not petition individual applications*"[64]. Therefore, public legal persons may not petition individual application or become a party to the individual application in our law. The reason is that public legal persons exercise public power and they represent the public authority. The fact that public legal persons exercise public power on one hand, and that they complain against the public power on the

---

63 As a matter of fact, the Court declined an application petitioned by an association to protect the right and benefits of the members of the association due to the "lack of jurisdiction *ratione personae*", see. AYM 1.Bl. Application Nr:2012/95, Application Date: 25.12.2012: http://www.anayasa.gov.tr/index.php?l= manage_k (date of accession: 22.07.2013).

64 An annulment action was filed against this provision on the grounds that the said provision is unconstitutional as Article 148 of the Constitution includes the phrase "everyone" and this provision brings new limitation which are not included therein. This annulment action was rejected with the decision of the Constiutional Court Nr. E.2011/59, K.201234, dated 1.3.2013. "*The texts of constitutions include general and abstract normp. Although the right to* individual application in Article 148 seems to be a right granted to everyone, it must be accepted that the content of the phrase "everyone" as it is included in the Constitution contains in itself some limitations arising from the characteristics personp.

other hand would be an oxymoron in itself. Therefore, the legislative organ adopted that the public legal persons may not petition individual application.

The rule that the public legal persons may not petition individual application is formulated in our law in definite terms so as not to leave any room for exceptions. Accordingly, a municipality, for instance, may not petition an individual application even when its freedom to claim right and right to a fair trial under Article 36 or principle of natural judge under Article 37 of the Constitution have been violated. On the other hand, although it is recognized in principle that the public legal persons do not possess legal capacity with regards to individual application (constitutional complaint) in German law, certain exceptions are brought to this rule. For instance, such institutions as universities, faculties, radios or churches which are relatively independent of the state are recognized to be entitled to lodge individual application (constitutional complaint) on the basis of certain fundamental rights due to the legal duties assigned to them. Similarly, political parties are entitled to petition individual application with regards to equal treatment to all political parties, as this issue is considered different from their constitutional status and to be relevant to their fundamental rights[65].

It is evident that public legal persons must have such fundamental rights as, especially, freedom to claim right, right to a fair trial and principle of natural judge in our law too. For that reason, it has been inappropriate to use a definite expression in Article 46, Paragraph 2 of the CCL which leaves no room for any exception. The Constitutional Court may bend this rule to a certain extent through its decisions and interpretations and satisfy the need to arise on this issue.

3 – Legal Capacity to be a Party is a Condition for Individual Application

Similar to the conditions of a lawsuit, the fact that the person to petition individual application has legal capacity is a condition for the individual application[66]. For that reason, the Constitutional Court (the commissions in principle) must *ex officio* observe whether the applicant possesses the legal capacity or not while examining the individual applications. If the applicant lacks legal capacity, the application must be declared inadmissible without further examining the merits of the application. However, as a requirement of the judicial economy and if it is possible to correct the deficiencies, it would be appropriate to give extra time to the applicant to correct those deficiencies before declaring the application inadmissible and to declare the application inadmissible if said deficiencies are not corrected in due time.

It must be recognized that the phrase "everyone" in Article 148 of the Constitution is not meant to include public legal persons exercising public power and that the legislative organ has discretionary power on this issue to determine those entitled to petition individual application.

Individual application mechanism is neither an ordinary legal remedy nor a remedy for the protection of all rights and freedoms secured under the Constitution. Therefore, it has different characteristics from those of the right to legal remedies under Article 36 of the Constitution. The right to legal remedies under Article 36 of the Constitution regulates the protective function of the general courts while the individual application is designed as a more special, exceptional and subsidiary legal remedy. Therefore the term "everyone" under Article 36 and the term "everyone" under Article 148 must be interpreted in accordance with the characteristics and nature of the legal remedies regulated under the relevant Article." http://www.anayasa.gov.tr/index.php?l= manage_k (date of accession: 22.07.2013).

65   Göztepe –Şikayet, p. 55-56.

66   As it was discussed above (§.1,B,II), individual application is not a luawsuit, therefore, we do not use the term "cause of action" we preferred the phrase "condition for the individual application" considering that it may assume the same function.

II – Capacity to Lodge Individual Application (Complaint)

Capacity to lodge individual application[67] is the legal capacity of a person to petition an individual application and follow the necessary proceedings either by himself or through an attorney to be appointed by him.

According to Article 9 *et al.* of the Civil Code, real and legal persons possessing capacity to act also have the capacity to individual application. Accordingly, capacity to individual application is an extension and a manifestation of the capacity to act. Therefore, one should possess the capacity to act in principle in order to have the capacity to individual application.

According to a view[68], "*the law does not stipulate the capacity to sue or be sued or the capacity to act of the procedural law for a person to petition an individual application; but states that "everyone" may apply. …there seems to be no limitation for a minor or a person lacking capacity to sue or be sued, to petition an individual application without the consent of the guardian. Seeking the capacity to sue or be sued of the procedural laws for the individual application too may lead to problems regarding the right to apply to the court. On the other hand, it is evident that the limitations imposed on the ways of petitioning an individual application will practically prevent the application of those lacking capacity to act.*" In my opinion, it is not possible to agree with this view. Although there is no provision in the law which explicitly states that those to petition individual application must also possess the capacity to act or there is no reference made to the relevant provisions of the Civil Code, it cannot be concluded solely on this ground that the capacity to individual application (comparing to the capacity to sue or be sued) is not stipulated at all for those to petition individual application. First of all, Article 49, Paragraph 7 of the CCL includes the provision of "*In the examination of individual applications, provisions of relevant procedural laws which relate to the individual application are applied in cases for which no provisions are laid down in this present Law and the Internal Regulation*"; a similar rule is also present in Article 81 of the Internal Regulation. In accordance with this provision, the relevant procedural law for the capacity to individual application is the Code of Civil Procedure. Article 50 of the Code of Civil Procedure regulates the contractual capacity and Article 51 regulates the capacity to sue or be sued. Accordingly, with reference to Article 49,7 of the CCL, the relevant provisions of the Code of Civil Procedure should be applied with regards to capacity to individual application for which no provisions are laid down in the CCL.

Just as the case in filing a lawsuit, certain rights and duties come out here with regards to the applicant and, if the application is rejected, a fine may be imposed on the applicant, in case of an abuse is determined by the Court, in addition to the cost of proceedings (Article 50 of the CCL). If we are to agree on this view, will the individual application filed by a person lacking capacity to appeal be accepted? If such a person petitions an application, will that fine penalty be imposed on him as well? It is impossible to give positive answers to these questions. Besides, the principle that the non-competent persons cannot apply on their own but apply through their legal attorneys, is adopted not to narrow down but to protect their rights. For that reason, one should possess the capacity to act in principle in order to have the capacity to individual application. However,

---

67 For the causes stated above in footnote 67, we preferred to use "capacity to individual application" instead of the capacity to sue or be sued.

68 Doğru – Bireysel Başvuru p. 99-100.

although the individual application mechanism is similar to a lawsuit, it is not identical to a lawsuit with all its characteristics[69]. Therefore, it may not always be possible to match up the capacity to individual application with the capacity to sue or be used. In principle, those who possess the capacity to sue or be used also have the capacity to individual application. Nevertheless, due to the specific characteristics of the individual application, it may be required under exceptional circumstances to recognize that those who do not possess the full capacity to sue or be sued, but capable of exercising their rights and freedoms independently may also have the capacity to individual application. The petitioning of an individual application by a person against a court decision on his confinement is an example for such application. Under such circumstances, the Court must hold the boundaries of the individual application broader, taking the particularities of the individual application into consideration. However, such cases are of exceptional nature. They cannot be extended to the general principles and it can not be concluded that capacity to individual application (capacity to act or capacity to sue or be sued) is not a requirement to petition individual application and that no limitation is imposed on this matter

As the status of the real persons and legal persons are different with regards to the capacity to lodge individual application, it would be appropriate to examine them separately.

1 – Real Persons

According to Article 10 of the Civil Code, "*every adult person possessing distinguishing power and not in the state of disability is deemed to possess full legal capacity*". Accordingly, every adult person possessing distinguishing power and not in the state of disability has the capacity to act, and hence, the capacity to lodge individual application. Nevertheless, as the individual application is not identical to an ordinary lawsuit, it would be appropriate, especially in the case of an individual application against a court decision, to examine whether the applicant alone has the capacity to exercise the right constituting the subject matter of that decision.

Those entitled to lodge individual application may apply either in person or through an attorney . Minors and disabled persons with distinguishing power (TCC Article 16, Paragraph 1) do not have the capacity to act and, hence, the capacity to lodge individual application in principle. However, as they are recognized to possess the capacity to act under certain circumstances in accordance with the Civil Code, they must also be recognized to have capacity to individual application under such circumstances. Accordingly, minors and disabled persons with distinguishing power have the capacity to act and, hence, the capacity to lodge individual application in exercise of rights strictly bound to them (Article 16, Paragraph 1 of the TCC) and with regards to the rights and properties on which they have exclusive discretion (Articles 359 and 355 of the TCC). If the disabled person is granted the consent to engage in a profession or arts by the civil court of peace, or if a minor is granted such a consent by his custodian, these persons also have the capacity to act and, hence, the capacity to lodge individual application with regards to the acts and proceedings relating to such profession or arts (Articles 359 and 453 of the TCC). For instance, if a minor possessing distinguishing power objects against being placed under the guardianship, it must be recognized that such a minor has the capacity to individual application against that proceeding.

---

69   See. above. §.1,B,II.

Except for such circumstances stated above, the minors and disabled persons with distinguishing power do not have the capacity to lodge individual applications. They can petition individual applications only through their legal representatives.

Those for whom a representative guardian is appointed under Article 426 of the Turkish Civil Code, and those for whom an administrative guardian is appointed under Articles 427 and 428 do not have the capacity to lodge individual application with regards to the issues requiring the appointment of a guardian. If an individual application is to be petitioned with regards to the subject within the scope of guardian's duty, the application must be filed by the guardian.

Those who are lack of distinguishing power do not have the capacity to act as well (Article 14 of the Turkish Civil Code). Therefore, they do not have the capacity to lodge individual application either. If those who are lack of distinguishing power are required to petition an individual application, their legal representatives shall file the application on their behalf. .

2 – Legal Persons

Legal persons also have the capacity to act and, hence, the capacity to lodge individual application. However, as it was mentioned above, private law legal persons may petition individual applications whereas Article 46, Paragraph 2 of the CCL states that public legal persons may not petition individual application. Private law legal persons attain the capacity to act whenever they get established under the prevailing laws and as set out in incorporation documents (Article 49 or the TCC). Private law legal persons also become eligible to petition individual application by attaining the capacity to act. They exercise the capacity to lodge individual application through their organs authorized to represent them (Article 50 of the TCC; Article 52 of the CCP). Under these circumstances, public legal persons could also possess the capacity to individual application. However, as it was explained above, Article 46, Paragraph 2 of the CCL prohibits the petitioning of individual application by public legal entities. In this respect, it would not have any practical meaning or effect for the public legal persons to have the capacity to individual application. However, similar to the case in German Law, if certain public legal persons were granted the right to petition individual application with regards to the fundamental rights relating to their duties, it could have a practical meaning or effect for the public legal persons to have the capacity to lodge individual applications.

3 – Capacity to Lodge Individual Application is a Condition for Individual Application

Just like the legal capacity, the capacity to lodge individual application is a condition for individual application. Therefore, while examining the individual application petitions, the Constitutional Court (the commissions in principle) must *ex officio* observe whether the applicant possesses the capacity to lodge individual application or not. If the applicant lacks the capacity of individual application, then the application must be declared inadmissible without further examining the merits of the case. However, as a requirement of the judicial economy and if it is possible to correct the deficiencies, it would be appropriate to give extra time to the applicant to correct those deficiencies before declaring the application inadmissible, e.g. granting extra time to the guardian to inform whether he approves the individual application petitioned by the disabled person, and to further examine the merits of the case if said deficiencies are corrected in due time or declare the application inadmissible otherwise.

C – Foreigners

The legislative organ recognized that the foreigners may also petition individual application in principle and laid down the provision of Article 46, Paragraph 3 of the CCL *"foreigners may not petition individual applications concerning rights exclusive to Turkish citizens."* Accordingly, the foreigner may petition individual application if the rights granted to them have been violated. However, they may not lodge individual applications on the grounds that rights exclusive to Turkish citizens have been violated.

The legislative organ has recognized that foreigners who are subject to the public power of the Republic of Turkey may benefit from the fundamental rights and freedoms as and accorded them the right to lodge individual application. However, unlike the Turkish citizens, as the foreigners may not benefit from all fundamental rights and freedoms secured under the Constitution but may benefit only from those accorded to foreigners. Their entitlement to individual application has been restricted to such rights and freedoms that they can benefit from.

Article 16 of the Constitution reads as follows: "…*the fundamental rights and freedoms in respect to aliens may be restricted by law compatible with international law.*" In accordance with this provision, the foreigners may not enjoy unrestricted benefit from the rights and freedoms which are drawn up in the Constitution in fashion that encompasses the foreigners as well and usually regulated as rights and freedoms from which "everyone" may enjoy. The legislative body may further restrict exercise of such rights and freedoms by law. However, such restrictions to be imposed by law must be compatible with international law. For instance, Article 35, Paragraph 1 of the Constitution regulating the right to property reads: "*Everyone has the right to own and inherit property*". As it says "everyone" in the provision, the foreigner may exercise this right as well. However, the legislative body may, taking the rights and interests of the Republic of Turkey into consideration, impose restrictions on the acquisition of real property by the foreigners in Turkey. According to Article 16 of the Constitution, if the exercise of a right or freedom by the foreigners is restricted by law, the foreigners are obliged to obey such restriction. Therefore, they can petition an individual application within bounds of that restriction, if any of their rights and freedoms have been violated. Accordingly, if the acquisition of real property by the foreigners in a certain region have been prohibited or restricted to a certain amount by law or the decree of the Council of Ministers, such foreigners can petition individual application within bounds of that restriction on the grounds that their rights and freedoms have been violated.

In that case, foreigners may not petition individual applications concerning rights and freedoms granted exclusively to Turkish citizens under the Constitution. If any of the rights and freedoms that the foreigners are allowed to enjoy has been violated, such foreigners may petition individual applications against that violation within bounds of restrictions imposed by law.

In accordance with the restrictions explained above, foreign private law legal persons may apply solely on the grounds that their rights concerning legal personality have been violated just as it is for the Turkish private law legal persons (e.g. violation of the right to a fair trial in a case where a foreign company is a party before a Turkish court (Article 36 of the Constitution)).

D – Representation in individual application

Anyone possessing the capacity to lodge individual application may petition his application either in person or through a representative or an attorney appointed by him. Our law does not mandate to hire an attorney in order to petition an individual application. It is up to the will of the applicant whether to hire an attorney or not.

If the applicant wants to be represented by a representative, the person to be authorized must have the power of attorney and must also be registered in the bar association (Article 35 of Attorney's Act). This must be considered as a condition for individual application. Those who do not have the capacity to be attorney to the case may not petition individual application acting as the representative of an applicant and may not further follow individual application proceedings before the Court. For the applications petitioned through an attorney, the Court must *ex officio* observe whether the attorney possesses the capacity to represent the applicant or not. If the representative lacks such capacity, the application must be declared inadmissible. However, before declaring the application inadmissible, the Court must allow a reasonable period of time for the actual applicant to attest whether he consents to this application filed on his behalf or not. The application must be further examined if the applicant gives consent in due time. However, if the applicant does not give such consent, it would be appropriate to declare the application inadmissible.

If the applicant wants to be represented by an attorney, he must give a power of attorney to his lawyer. Such power of attorney may be issued or certified by a notary like in lawsuit cases. In my opinion, the general authorization furnished to the attorney relating to the case may not suffice and such a power of attorney to be given to the representative must also contain a special authorization for the petitioning of the individual application. Because, individual application is not a remedy that serves as a continuation of the lawsuit but a separate extraordinary legal remedy. In that case, the authorization granted for the lawsuit should not be considered adequate. Secondly, according to Article 51 of the CCL, applicants who are established to have clearly abused the right of individual application may be required to pay fine not more than 2000 Turkish Liras. For that reason, it would be appropriate to seek special authorization so that the client calls attorney's special attention to such a risk of monetary fine. However, it is seen in practice that such a special authorization is not sought in individual applications petitioned through an attorney with a view to ease the application process for the individuals.

In the applications petitioned through a representative, the name and surname, address, profession, if available the phone number and e-mail address must be stated in the application form (Article 59,2/c of the Internal Regulations). The original text and a certified copy of the power of attorney must also be submitted together with the application form (Article 47,4 of the CCL; Articles 59,3/a and 61,1 of the Internal Regulations). This issue must also be *ex officio* observed by the Court as a condition for the individual application.

If the power of attorney is not submitted together with the individual application form, the Individual Applications Bureau shall allow a time period not exceeding fifteen days to the attorney of the applicant as *per* Article 66 of the Internal Regulations. If the original or a certified copy of the power of attorney is submitted in due time, the application will be further examined or it will be declared inadmissible otherwise.

In applications petitioned through an attorney, the correspondences with the attorney or the notifications made to the attorney shall be deemed to have been served or notified to the applicant (Article 61,2 of the Internal Regulations; Article 11,1 of the Notifications Law).

§.5 – Admissibility criteria for the individual application

A – In general terms

We have mentioned above who may petition individual application for which rights and freedoms and the legal capacity and capacity to petition individual application required for the applicants. Except for these, there are some other criteria to petition an individual application in due form, or for the admissibility of the application already petitioned. Such criteria are explained in Article 46 *et al.* of the CCL. We have considered it appropriate to examine such criteria under two heading, one being material criteria and the other formal criteria. Because, such criteria as actuality, directness and legal interest which are related in terms of material law to the link between the applicant and the relevant right. On the other hand, some of those criteria are related to formal or procedural issues such as application in due time and exhaustion of legal remedies.

B – Material criteria

Material criteria required for the admissibility of the individual application may be stated as follows: 1- Violation of a personal right, 2- Direct influence, 3- Actuality of the right, 4- Existence of legal interest, 5- Significance for the enforcement and interpretation of the Constitution, 6- Significant damage sustained by the applicant, 7- Being manifestly ill-founded, 8- Nonexistence of an application in pending status relating to the same right, 9-Non-existence of a final decision relating to the same right. Article 46, Paragraph1 of the CCL regulates the first three criteria explicitly by stating *"Individual applications may only be filed by those whose actual and personal rights are directly affected by the alleged proceeding, act or negligence which has caused the violation."* Similarly, Article 48, Paragraph 2 includes the 5th, 6th and 7th criteria by stating *"The Court may dismiss applications which do not bear significance for the enforcement and interpretation of the Constitution, or for the determination of the scope and limits of fundamental rights, applications which do not require meritorious decisions and which do not involve significant damage sustained by the applicant."*

Now, we would like to examine these criteria closely.

I – Violation of a Personal Right

The right alleged to have been violated must be a personal right of the applicant petitioning the individual application. The applicant may petition an application only if one of his/her personal and fundamental rights and freedoms have been violated; he/she may not petition an application on the grounds that the rights of another person (real or legal) have been violated.

As it is seen, this criterion questions the relation between the violated right and the holder of that right. As a requirement of this criterion, there must be a material "holder of right" relationship between the applicant and the rights alleged to have been violated. In other terms, the fundamental right or freedom alleged to have been violated must belong to the applicant himself/herself.

Due to this criterion, a private law legal person may petition an individual application only when its own fundamental rights and freedoms have been violated[70]; it may not lodge an application for the common interest of its members. As a matter of fact, this situation is stated separately in Article 46, Paragraph 2 of the CCL *"Private-law legal persons may apply solely on the grounds that their rights concerning legal personality have been violated."*

We have already examined under the legal capacity heading what the outcome of an application will be if the applicant dies after petitioning the application[71]. Those such as bankruptcy offices, trustees in composition or testamentary executors who are party to a case or a legal relationship as a requirement of their duty, may petition an individual application when it is required within the scope of their duties and responsibilities.

As individual applications may not be petitioned against legislative proceedings and regulatory administrative proceedings in our law, it is not principally necessary to re-examine whether a right of the individual have been violated or not. On the other hand, in Germany for instance, individual application may be petitioned against the laws violating a personal right and it may require a serious examination to determine whether a provision of law violates a personal right or not.

When an individual application is petitioned against the personal proceedings of the administration or against the court decisions, it is easier to determine whether the applicant's personal right has been violated or not. It is natural that the personal rights of the parties to the proceeding or the case may be affected by the decision given. Similarly, under certain conditions and although they are not a party to the case, the rights of the third parties such as secondary intervening parties may have been violated as well and they can petition an individual application for their such rights.

II – Direct Influence

This criterion is related to which proceeding of public power affects the right alleged by the applicant to have been violated. The right alleged by the applicant to have been violated must be directly violated by an act or proceeding of the public power. In other words, the violation must be caused by the act or proceeding stated in the application not by any other act or proceeding of the public power. If the alleged violation is caused by any act or proceeding of the public power other than the one stated in the application, then the condition for direct influence is not satisfied. Accordingly, there must be a direct cause and effect relationship established between the allegedly violated right and the proceeding of the public power. If another proceeding of the

---

70   Oder, Bertil Emrah: Anayasa Mahkemesine Bireysel Başvuruda (Anayasa Şikayeti) Etkin ve Etkili Kullanım Sorunları: HUKAB Sempozyum Serisi 1, Bireysel Başvuru "Anayasa Şikayeti" Ankara 2011, p. 95.

71   Bkz. yuk. §.4,B,I,1.

administration is intervening to cause the said violation result, then that proceeding must be stated as the subject of individual application.

This criterion has greater importance in countries such as Germany where individual application may be petitioned against the laws as well[72]. As individual applications may not be petitioned against legislative proceedings and regulatory administrative proceedings in our law, the scope of application for this criterion may remain quite limited[73]. Because, when it comes to the proceedings of the administration or the court decisions, it is much easier to determine that the fundamental right alleged to have been violated is directly influenced by the proceeding or the court decision.

III – Actuality of the Right

According to Article 46, Paragraph 1 of the CCL ""Individual applications may only filed by those whose actual and personal rights are directly affected." In that case, in order to petition an individual application, personal right of the applicant must be violated and such right must be in actual status as of the date of application. On this issue, the actuality of the right is related to the persistence of the effect of the violation on one hand and the legal interest on the other hand[74].

First of all, it must be stated that either the proceeding of the public power itself or, if such act or proceeding has ceased to exist, its effects violating the right of the applicant must be in existence at the time of application. Individual application may not be petitioned on the grounds of violating a personal right against a proceeding of the public power which ceased to exist and no longer has an effect violating the said right.

Secondly, the personal right of the applicant alleged to have been violated must still be in actual status as of the time of individual application. That right must still be claimable and in possession of the applicant; there must be a restriction or an unfavorable condition in the legal status or fundamental rights and freedoms of the applicant due to the violation alleged and such unfavorable condition must be still continuing.

Thirdly, acting on the wording of Article 46, Paragraph 1 of the CCL and Article 148, Paragraph 3 of the Constitution, it can be concluded that the fundamental rights must have already been violated in order to lodge an individual application and that an application may not be filed for a potential violation of right possible to happen in future. It can be said that the legislative organ, taking the possible workload to arise with individual application into consideration, did not prefer the petitioning of individual application for potential violation of rights and, hence, preferred such a legislative regulation model. However, it must be accepted that such a result would contradict with the practices of the European Court of Human Rights, which accepts the application for potential violation of rights within certain limits[75].

Indeed, the criterion for actuality may have a field of implementation for the personal proceedings of the administration and court decisions which are recognized to be subject to

---

72   See. Göztepe – Şikayet p. 62-65.
73   Oder p. 95-96.
74   Göztepe – Şikayet p. 65.
75   Oder p. 95.

individual application. However, this condition bears greater importance in countries where individual application may be petitioned against the provisions of the law. As direct individual applications may not be petitioned against legislative proceedings in our country, we will not examine this issue in details.

IV – Existence of Legal Interest

The criterion for the legal interest of the applicant while petitioning an individual application is not stated separately under the CCL. However, the fact that it is not stated in the law does not mean that the legal interest of the applicant in petitioning the application will not be sought. As it is known, legal interest is sought after as a cause of action in other law cases. As a matter of fact, Article 114/1-h of the Code of Civil Procedure states this fact explicitly. Legal interest must be sought in petitioning an individual application as it is required in filing a lawsuit[76].

Accordingly, when requesting for an aid or legal protection from the Constitutional Court, the applicant must have a legal interest worthy of protection[77]. The fact that the applicant possesses the capacity to lodge individual application or the capacity to complain against public power is not sufficient alone; there must be a legal interest in the application as well[78]. A person who does not have a legal interest in petitioning an individual application is expected not to engage the Constitutional Court unnecessarily.

The criterion for the legal interest is, indeed, also connected with the above-mentioned condition of "the violation of an actual and personal right". Generally, if an actual and personal right of the applicant has been violated, then it can be considered that there is legal interest in elimination of such a violation[79].However, this issue may be different in each case and, therefore, it must be separately examined whether there is a legal interest or not. For instance, if the applicant has petitioned an application against an administrative proceeding violating his personal right and such violation has been eliminated by the administration's abolishing of the mentioned proceeding; then there is no more legal interest in petitioning an individual application against such proceeding.

The criterion of legal interest is closely related to the criteria of the exhaustion of legal remedies and the individual application's subsidiary status which we will examine in details below. Accordingly, if the violation of a right subject to individual application can be redressed through any other legal remedy prescribed by law, e.g. by fling a lawsuit, way of appeal, then individual application may not be petitioned as there is no legal interest of the applicant in such an application[80]. Similarly, the applicant does not have any legal interest in principle in petitioning an individual application on the grounds of a case on trial.

The criterion of the legal interest should not be interpreted as it is in other cases, especially the civil cases. The nature and the purpose of the individual application mechanism must be taken into consideration and the legal interest must be determined accordingly. If the violation

---

76 Ekinci p. 142-143.
77 Karş. Kuru/Arslan/Yılmaz – Usul p. 261.
78 Atasoy. p. 80; Kılınç p. 92.
79 Göztepe-Şikayet p. 67.
80 Sabuncu/Arnwine-Esen p. 232; Ekinci p. 142; Aliyev p. 21.

of a right by the public power proceeding can be determined through individual application and the expected legal protection can be afforded by ensuring the new trial for court decisions or by awarding due compensation, then it means that the applicant has legal interest.

However, as the individual application is not a mechanism which is adopted to ensure substantial justice in principle, certain restrictions have been imposed as well. According to Article 48, Paragraph 2 of the CCL, the Court may dismiss applications which do not bear significance for the enforcement and interpretation of the Constitution or for the determination of the scope and limits of fundamental rights, applications which are manifestly ill-founded and which do not involve significant damage sustained by the applicant. Therefore, the legal interests of the applicant under such conditions have been ignored or disregarded by the legislative organ.

The commissions or the sections in charge of examining the individual applications must *ex officio* search the criterion of legal interest in each stage of the trial. According to the provision of Article 80,1-c of the Internal Regulations, the decision of dismissal may be given if the said violation and its effects have been removed[81]. However, even when the violation of right and its effects have been removed, the sections or the commissions may continue their examination of the case if it bears significance for the enforcement and interpretation of the Constitution or for the determination of the scope and limits of fundamental rights, or if it is a requirement of the respect for human rights (Internal Regulations Art. 80, Paragraph 2). As it is seen, the nature of the individual application requires under certain conditions the examination of certain applications by the Court even when personal legal interest of the applicant no longer exists.

---

81 AYM 2. Bl,. Application Nr: 2013/463, Decision dated 16.5.2013 ".....

13. The applicant stated that his request to extract the MERNIS and SGK records of the debtor through UYAP with regards to the file nr. 2012/12547 at 30th Execution Office of Ankara, where he initiated the execution proceedings through his lawyer, was rejected on the grounds that the request was made by the lawyer; that such requests related to the execution proceedings initiated and followed directly by the creditors are accepted by the execution offices while there is a different practice in procedures followed through a lawyer. The applicant alleged that such a practice violates the principal of equality and right to a fair trial and right to legal remedies under Article 10 and Article 36 of the Constitution. The applicant demanded that the said Court decision and its results be ruled out.

17. It is seen in the case subject to application that the allegation of violation is based on the grounds that 30th Execution Office of Ankara rejected the applicant's request to extract the MERNIS and SGK records of the debtor through UYAP as the procedures were initiated and followed by a lawyer and restricted the applicant's right to access such addresses. However, it is seen that the lawyer can access such information easily over UYAP in accordance with the protocol signed between the Ministry of Justice and, Turkish Bar Association and, if he is not capable of doing so, that it is always possible to have the address determined through execution office or the municipal police by paying the related expenses

18. *Furthermore, it is understood from the letter of the 30th Execution Office dated 16/5/2013 that the applicant himself accessed the addresses he wanted and that the applicant demanded on 8/11/2012 a notification be sent to the address declared by the attorney of the debtor. This request for notification was accepted by the Execution Office and a notification was sent to the said addres, an attachment order was levied on the motor wehicle belonging to the debtor and a warrant for the garnishment of wages was issued. As it is understtod that the information requested by the attorney of the applicant such as the address and the garnishable assets of the debtor could be accessedeasily, there was no justification for the continuation of the examination on the application. Therefore, the application was dropped out in accordance with Article 80 of the Internal Regulations sub-caluse (ç) of Paragraph (1)."* http://www.anayasa.gov.tr/index.php?l= manage_k (date of accession: 22.07.2013)

V – Constitutional Significance of the Application

Article 48, Paragraph 2 of the CCL reads *"The Court may dismiss applications which do not bear significance for the enforcement and interpretation of the Constitution or for the determination of the scope and limits of fundamental rights, ... and which do not involve significant damage sustained by the applicant."* Accordingly, the violation of a personal and actual right of the applicant is not sufficient for the admission of the application. The application must also be constitutionally "significant". The scope of such significance is explained in the law by stating *"...bear significance for the enforcement and interpretation of the Constitution or for the determination of the scope and limits of fundamental rights"*.

Following points may be stated relating to the conditions for the constitutional significance of the application[82]:

- That no previous decision has been given by the Constitutional Court relating to the violation of fundamental right in question by the public power and that the decision to be given will be of precedential nature,
- Although there is an already established case-law of the Constitutional Court on a subject matter, the need to review and change such case-law in light of the subsequent circumstances and causes,
- Although there is an already established case-law of the Constitutional Court on a subject matter, the systematic neglect of such case-law by other judicial authorities,
- That the violation subject matter to application amounts to a serious extent and has substantial effects on the applicant.
- That many persons other than the applicant of the concrete case may also benefit form the decision to be given, e.g. if the unconstitutionality of a law provision is to be reviewed due to an application, others may have benefit in such a review as well[83].

According to Article 80 of the Internal Regulations, an application can be dismissed in case of the explicit withdrawal of the applicant from the case, understanding that the applicant has no intention to proceed his application, or the alleged violation and its consequences have been removed, and owing to any other justification determined by sections or commissions finding no cause which justifies the continuation of examination of the application. However, even under such conditions, the sections or the commissions may continue their examination of the case if it bears significance for the enforcement and interpretation of the Constitution or for the determination of the scope and limits of fundamental rights or if it a requirement of the respect for human rights

VI – Significant Damage Sustained by the Applicant

Article 48, Paragraph 2 of the CCL states that application may be dismissed if the applicant did not sustain a significant damage. The legislative organ intended this criterion to be fulfilled together with the above-described condition of constitutional significance and, for that reason,

---

82 Ekinci/Sağlam p. 24-25.
83 Göztepe – Şikayet p. 80; F. Sağlam – Anayasa Şikayeti p. 86 et al.

used "and" conjunction instead of "or" in the wording of the provision. In that case, in addition to the constitutional significance of the application, the damage sustained by the applicant must also be a significant one[84]. In other words, the infringement or violation caused by the public power proceeding should not be at insignificant, slight or reasonably bearable level but must amount to a significant level.

VII – Not Being Manifestly Ill-founded

According to Article 48, Paragraph 2 of the CCL, "*The Court may dismiss applications … which are manifestly ill-founded.*" According to this provision, an application shall not be manifestly ill-founded to be declared admissible by the Court. Applications which are manifestly ill-founded are rejected at the phase of admissibility examination on the grounds that they are "manifestly ill-founded". The condition of being manifestly ill-founded may be applicable if it is explicitly understood that the alleged violation of right does not exist or its existence can not be proved, if the said proceeding of the public power alleged to have caused violation does not exist or that the said proceeding is legal and legitimate[85]. As for the applications against the court decisions, it may be applicable if the application is petitioned based on the matters to be observed in the " appeal ways".

By obliging the applications not to be manifestly ill-founded, the legislative organ aimed to prevent the engagement of the Constitutional Court with dismissive applications.

VIII – Non-Existence of a Final Decision

If an application was previously petitioned on the fundamental right subject to application and a decision was given by the commissions or sections, such a decision constitutes a final decision for a second application to be petitioned on the same subject matter. There must not be a previously given decision on the right subject matter to the application. If there is such a final decision, the section or the commission must reject the application on that ground[86].

In order to mention the existence of a final decision on the right subject matter to the application; the applicants, subject matter and the public power proceeding causing the violation must be identical both in the final decision and the second application.

IX – Non-Existence of an Application in Pending Status

Application in pending status means that the Court is still examining the application and that the trial is continuing. Pending status begins with the petitioning of the individual application. A second application on the same issue must not be lodged. If such an application is petitioned, the second application shall be rejected on the grounds that the first application is in pending

---

84 Çoban p. 173-174.
85 Çoban p. 172.
86 Atasoy p. 82; Gören, Zafer: Anayasa Şikayeti: Külfetsiz, Masrafsız ve Sonuçsuz ?: Prof. Dr. Ergun Özbudun'a Armağan, Cilt II, Ankara 2008, p. 319.

status. Indeed, the applicant has no legal interest in re-petitioning his application notwithstanding the pending status of his first application.

With regards to the pending status of the individual application, it makes no difference whether the application is in examination of admissibility at the commissions or in substantial examination on merits at the sections.

Like in the criterion of the final decision, in order to mention the existence of a pending status; the applicants, subject matters and the public power proceeding causing the violation must be identical both in the pending application and the second application.

C – Formal Criteria

I – The Proceedings and Decisions Subject to Application Must be Final before the Date of 23.09.2012

According to the provision of Article 76/1-a of the CCL, Articles 45-41 regulating the individual application enter into force on the date of 23.09.2012. According to provisional Article 1/8 of the said Law, "*The Court deals with individual applications filed against final proceedings and decisions which become final and notified after 23/9/2012*". Accordingly, the *ratione temporis* of the Constitutional Court starts from the date of 23.09.2012 and is valid for proceedings and decisions which are finalized after that date. Individual application may not be petitioned against proceedings and especially against the court decisions finalized before that date[87].

It is possible that the act or proceeding subject matter to the application may have happened before the date of 23.09.2012 and a case may have been filed against such proceeding. What's important here is, especially if a case is filed, that the decision given in the result of the trial must be finalized after the date of 23.09.2012. In this context, if an application was made for a legal remedy, e.g. way of appeal, before the date of 23.09.2012 against the relevant court decision and, subsequently, the final high court decision was given after the date of 23.09.2012; individual application may be petitioned against such a decision. On the other hand, if the decision in the result of the legal remedy was given before the date of 23.09.2012 and ordinary legal remedies were exhausted, individual application may not be petitioned then.

II – Exhaustion of Administrative and Judicial Remedies

According to Article 45,2 of the CCL "*All administrative and judicial remedies provided by the law relating to the proceeding, act or negligence which is alleged to have caused violation must be exhausted prior to individual application.*" As it is seen, the law explicitly regulates that the remedies prescribed within the judicial system for the elimination of the violation must be exhausted prior to individual application.

An annulment action was filed at the Constitutional Court against these clauses which prescribe the exhaustion of administrative and judicial remedies on the grounds that they are

---

87   Özbey p. 149.

ambiguous and may lead to confusion. This annulment action was rejected by the Court on the following grounds:

"Individual application is neither an appellate remedy nor a new legal remedy to claim the elimination of illegalities to have occurred in judicial, administrative or military justice. Individual application is a legal remedy through which individuals whose constitutional rights have been violated by a proceeding of the public power may claim the elimination of such a violation. As the administrative and judicial authorities have a more efficient position in the prevention of the violations of human rights, it is primarily the duty and responsibility of all administrative and judicial authorities to prevent such violations. Therefore, Article 148 of the Constitution and Article 45 of the CCL obliges the applicants to apply to the relevant authorities for the elimination of such violations before petitioning an application to the Constitutional Court. Furthermore, as the individual application is an extraordinary legal remedy, it is laid down that individual application may be petitioned to the Constitutional Court only if all administrative and judicial remedies have been exhausted and the violation of a fundamental right can not still be removed.

The requirement for the prior exhaustion of administrative remedies in addition to the judicial remedies expresses an order to be observed in the sequence of the remedies. It is evident that the nature of the process requires applying to the administrative remedies before legal remedies for the elimination of the violation.

Furthermore, constitutional provisions are inherently general and abstract norms which need to be concretized by laws. The criterion of "the exhaustion of ordinary legal remedies" to be satisfied before petitioning an individual application is laid down by Article 148 of the Constitution and Article 45,2 of the CCL further clarifies this provision by stating that "ordinary legal remedies" of the constitutional provision means "administrative and judicial remedies provided by the law"[88]

This criterion is also closely related to the principle of the subsidiarity of individual application which will be discusses in details below.

The phrase of "administrative and judicial remedies" stipulated in the provision must be clarified. First of all, if there is a remedy within the administrative mechanism available against an administrative proceeding, e.g. objecting to a disciplinary punishment, such remedies must be applied and exhausted. If a court case can be filed against the act or proceeding of the public power violating the right[89], then that remedy must also be applied and exhausted.

If the individual application is petitioned against a court decision, other legal remedies provided by law against said court decision such as objection or appeal must be exhausted. The revision of decision mechanism in our law is an ordinary legal remedy that serves as a continuation of the appeal process. However, revision of decision mechanism has been decided to be abolished with the adoption of regional appeal process as a legal remedy and the Code of Civil Procedure Nr. 61000 does not include revision of decision mechanism as a legal remedy. However, it is prescribed that the provisions on the revision of decision mechanism (Article 440-44 of the Code of Civil Procedure) shall be exercised until the inauguration of the regional courts of appeal (Provisional Article 3 of the Code of Civil Procedure). For that reason, it would be

---

88   Decision of the Constitutional Court dated 1.3.2012, Nr. E.2011/59, K.2012/34: http://www.anayasa.gov.tr/index.php?l= manage_k (date of accession: 22.07.2013)

89   It should be noted that judicial remedies are available against all acts and proceedings of the administration in accordance with Article 125,1 of the Constitution.

beneficial to dwell briefly on the revision of decision mechanism as a legal remedy. As the "revision of decision" is an ordinary legal remedy, it could be prescribed mandatory to exhaust this remedy as well before petitioning an individual application. However, due to such facts as this legal remedy is not available in other judicial systems, there are limited justifications for revision of decision and that the Court of Cassation may impose a fine if the application is rejected, the European Court of Human Rights does not recognize the "revision of decision" mechanism as a domestic remedy which must be exhausted prior to applying to the Court. In accordance with this judicial opinion of the European Court of Human Rights, the Constitutional Court recognized that "revision of decision" does not have to be exhausted and individual application may be petitioned after the appeal procedure. However, if the applicant has applied to the revision of decision mechanism as a legal remedy, the individual applications to be petitioned later on in due time are also accepted.

If there are any legal remedies for the fulfillment of a right other than ordinary legal remedies described above as objection or appeal which fall into the scope of the "judicial remedies" prescribed under Article 45, Paragraph 2 of the CCL, e.g. reinstatement if a deadline is missed, such remedies must also be applied and exhausted.

Do the extraordinary legal remedies, such as motion for a new trial, have to be exhausted as well? There is no clear provision on this issue in the CCL. However, Article 148, Paragraph 3 of the Constitution explicitly states that ordinary legal remedies must be exhausted. Therefore, extraordinary legal remedies are not required to be exhausted prior to individual application. At a time when the conditions for an extraordinary legal remedy are not present yet and it is not definite whether the motion for a new trial can be filed or not, it would be contrary to the nature of the procedure and no legal interest may be expected of such a practice. If it is understood that the motion for a new trial can be filed and that the said violation of right can be eliminated through this remedy, then motion for a new trial must be applied. Individual application must be petitioned if the infringement of right is not eliminated after the exhaustion of that remedy.

If a legal remedy has already been applied, as a rule, individual application may not be petitioned before the conclusion of that legal remedy but application may be filed after the finalization of that legal remedy.

Article 45, Paragraph 2 of the CCL regulates the criteria of the exhaustion of administrative and judicial remedies in definite terms without leaving no room for any exception. However, the Federal Constitutional Court of Germany, for instance, has brought certain exceptions to this criterion in practice and did not require the exhaustion of legal remedies under certain circumstances. These circumstances can be summarized as follows: The exhaustion of legal remedies is not required -as an exception-, when no result is expected to be achieved through the exhaustion of legal remedies, when the individual application (constitutional complaint) has overall importance, when grave and irreparable damages are sustained by the applicant[90]. The case-law of the Constitutional Court will clarify whether such exceptions may be brought in the Turkish Law to the exhaustion of legal remedies[91].

What is meant with the exhaustion of administrative and judicial remedies before individual application as stipulated under Article 45, Paragraph 2 of the CCL is applied to such rem-

---

90   Sabuncu/Arnwine-Esen p. 232;Göztepe – Şikayet p. 78 et al.
91   Oder p. 102.

edies in due form but achieving no result to remove the said violation. If the applicant did not apply to the administrative and judicial remedies in due form, e.g. in due course of time, he would not be deemed to have exhausted the administrative and judicial remedies and his individual application shall not be accepted.

III – Subsidiarity of Individual Application

Individual application is of secondary (subsidiary) nature in eliminating the violation of fundamental rights and freedoms when compared to other legal remedies. Therefore, such characteristics of the individual application must be taken into consideration by both the applicants and the Constitutional Court, which will examine the individual applications. It must be noted that this matter is not explicitly stipulated in the CCL. However, depending on the above-mentioned criteria of the exhaustion of administrative and judicial remedies or as an extension of that criterion, it is accepted that the individual application bears a subsidiary nature in our law[92].

As the subsidiarity of the individual application is dependent on the principle of the exhaustion of administrative and judicial remedies, the scope is determined accordingly. The principle of the exhaustion of administrative and judicial remedies is intended to ensure the application and exhaustion of those remedies in formal terms but the principle of subsidiarity is related to the scope of the allegations of violation raised during the process of those legal remedies. The applicant must have asserted and raised the allegations of violation subject to individual application before the courts which carried out the trial proceedings or during the previous legal remedies applied. Accordingly, the protection of the fundamental rights and freedoms is essentially the duty of the administrative authorities, courts of first instance and highs courts upon application for legal remedies. If the violation of a right cannot be eliminated through such remedies, then individual application may be petitioned in that case. This principle defines the scope of duty for the Constitutional Court in examining the individual applications and it is decisive in determining the boundaries of the jurisdictional relations among other courts, especially high courts. As matter of fact, Article 148, Paragraph 4 of the Constitution indicates this point by stating *"In the individual application, judicial review shall not be made on matters required to be taken into account during the process of legal remedies."* Similarly, Article 50, Paragraph 1 of the CCL states that expediency review cannot be made and court decisions cannot be rendered in the form of an administrative act or decision during the examination of individual applications.

This principle confirms from a different standpoint that the individual application is an extraordinary legal remedy. As a matter of fact, the main duty and responsibility in the protection of fundamental rights and freedoms is assigned to the administrative authorities and to courts by recognizing the individual application as an extraordinary remedy. The aim of such a regulation is to reduce the workload of the Constitutional Court and thereby allocate more time to the constitutionality review of the legislation[93].

---

92   Atasoy p. 80; Özbey p. 74.
93   Göztepe – Şikayet p. 77; Atasoy p. 80.

IV – Time

1 – Application within 30 Days Period

According to Article 47, Paragraph 5.1 of the CCL "*The application must be filed within thirty days after the final proceeding which exhausts legal remedies is notified to the applicant or, in case no legal remedy is provided for, within thirty days after the violation is found out.*" Accordingly, a time period of 30 days is prescribed for the petitioning of the individual application. This time period is defined by law and, therefore, it can neither be changed nor extended. This thirty-day period is a final term. Accordingly, if an application is not filed within this thirty-day period, the right to petition an application will expire. The application to be filed after the expiration of this time period will be rejected solely on this ground.

If an administrative or legal remedy is provided against the public proceedings alleged to have caused the violation, this thirty day period shall begin from the date such remedies are exhausted and the decision is finalized and notified to the applicant[94]. For instance if an application is to be petitioned against a court decision, such decision must be brought for appeal and the time period must start from the date when the final decision of the High Court is notified to the applicant. Except for the notification, if the concerned party has learned the decision through pronouncing or announcement, then the time period may start from the date of pronouncing or announcement. If no legal remedy is prescribed against the public proceedings alleged to have violated a right, then the time period may start from the actual date on which the said violation was found out. For such a probability, the legislative body has not prescribed a maximum time period. Therefore, it seems that individual application may be petitioned even if the violation is found out years later. However, with regard to such a probability, it would be appropriate to set a specific maximum time period, e.g. one year, for such occasions.

If an individual application is to be petitioned against a negligence of the public power, application may be filed so long as the negligence persists. If the negligence no longer persists, it would be appropriate to start the thirty-day period from the date on which negligence ended[95].

Upon the applicant's petitioning his/her application duly to the authorities cited in the Law within due time duration, his/her application his registered and the applicant is provided with a voucher documenting the receipt of application. As the application is deemed to have been made on this registration date, adherence to the thirty-day period shall be calculated according to this date[96].

2 – Reinstatement[97]

According to sentence 2 and 3 of Article 47,5 of the CCL "*Those who fail to apply within due time as a consequence of a warranted excuse may apply within fifteen days after the excuse ceases to*

---

94 Although Article 64,1 of the Internal Regulation states that the application must be petitioned within 30 days after the decision becomes final, this time period must start not from the date of finalization but from the date of notification to the related person.

95 Göztepe-Şikayet p. 83.

96 Ekinci/Sağlam p. 26.

97 For Reinstatement in Law of Civil Procedure see. Tercan, Erdal: Medeni Usul Hukukunda (Kesin Sürelerin Kaçırılması Halinde) Eski Hale Getirme, Ankara 2006.

exist and must present evidence proving the excuse. The court examines validity of the excuse first and then either admits or dismisses the claim." Petition for reinstatement is accepted if the due time period of individual applications has been missed as a consequence of a warranted excuse. Article 64, Paragraph 2 of the Internal Regulations further explains the warranted excuse by stating "a warranted excuse such as a *force majeure* or severe disease".

The applicant must submit his petition for reinstatement within fifteen days after the excuse ceases to exist and must also attach the evidence proving the warranted excuse, e.g. medical report, accident report, to the petition for reinstatement. The applicant must submit both his for reinstatement and the petition for individual application at the same time.

The rapporteurs' office of the commissions first prepares a draft decision on the admissibility of the excuse. The commission examines validity of the excuse first and then either admits or dismisses the claim. (Article 64, Paragraph 2 of Internal Regulations). If the excuse is found admissible, the file is sent back to the rapporteur judge and he prepares a draft decision on the admissibility of the application. If it befits the nature of the application, a single draft shall be prepared for both the excuse and the admissibility and these two issues shall be decided jointly (Article 64, Paragraph 3 of Internal Regulations).

V – Payment of the Application Fee

The legislative body recognizes with Article 47, Paragraph 2 of the CCL that the individual application is subject to a fee. According to Article 62, Paragraph 1 of the Internal Regulations, the fee for individual application which is specified in the first sentence of the Section A) Court Fees under Tariff Nr.1 appended to Law of Fees Nr. 492 must be paid to the Treasury offices. Petitions for individual application may not be accepted without the payment of application fee. If it is understood that the application fee has not been paid or that it is under-paid, the applicant shall be granted fifteen-day duration to make the payment or to complement the missing amount. If the application fee is not paid within the time period allowed, the application shall be declared inadmissible. The application fee for the year 2015 is 226,90 TL (approximately 80 Euro). Legal aid mechanism is recognized for those who lack the economic means to pay the applications fee. The requests for legal aid shall also be decided in accordance with the general provisions by the sections or the commission which are to decide on the admissibility of the application itself. Legal aid mechanism is regulated in Articles 334-340 of the Code of Civil Procedure in principle and such provisions shall also find a field of application for the legal aid requests with regards to individual applications so long as they befit the nature of the mechanism.

VI – Application in Written

Article 47, Paragraph 3 of the CCL mentions a petition of application with regard to in what form the application shall be made. Articles 59 and 60 of the Internal Regulations state that the application shall be made by filling out the application form. In any case, the application shall be made in written. The applicant may apply with a separate petition which includes the points specified in Article 59, Paragraph 1 of the Internal Regulations or he may prefer to use the application form attached to the Internal Regulations and also available at the website of the

Court. Application form is designed as "fill-in the blanks" type for the ease of applicants. Practically all applications are petitioned via application form. The application must be petitioned in Turkish language.

The issues to be included in the application form are cited in Article 59, Paragraph 1 of the Internal Regulations. In addition to personal identifying information, the facts and events relating to the proceeding, act or negligence of the public power alleged to have caused the violation of a right, which right is violated and the grounds for the said violation, the basis for the allegation that an actual and personal right is directly affected and the claims of the of the applicant must be specified.

The original or certified copies of the supporting documents and, if there is any claim for damages, the documents relating to the damages sustained must be attached to the application. If the application form exceeds ten pages, an additional "summary of the facts" must also be added.

§.6 – Petitioning, review and resolving of the individual application

A – The units of the constitutional court in charge of individual Application and their duties

In order to better understand the petitioning, review and resolving of the individual applications, it would be appropriate to touch briefly upon the structure of the Constitutional Court, its units established for individual application and the duties of such units.

General Assembly: General Assembly is the board consisting of seventeen members and is held with the participation of all members. Except for the individual application proceedings, General Assembly deals with constitutionality review of the laws, statutory decrees and Internal Regulations of the Grand National Assembly, tries and conducts cases in its capacity as the Grand Court and carries out audits on political parties and performs other duties. General Assembly is presided over by the president to be elected among the members of the assembly. General Assembly also elects two vice-presidents. General assembly has no duty with regards to individual applications in principle. However, General Assembly resolves the possible conflicts arising from judicial opinion differences among the sections.

Sections: Sections are presided by a vice-president and each section is made up of seven members. Each section convenes and decides with five members including the vice-president. There are two sections which conduct the examination on the merits of the individual applications declared admissible by the commissions and conclude such applications. The sections also conduct both the examination of admissibility and examination on the merits of individual applications when a commission cannot render an admissibility decision (Article 22 of the CCL; Article 28 of the Internal Regulations).

Commissions: Each section having three commissions, there are six commissions in total. Each commission is made up of two members and examination for admissibility is conducted by these commissions. (Article 32 of the Internal Regulations).

Moreover, a large number of rapporteur judges are assigned to help the sections and commissions and to prepare draft decisions.

B – Petitioning of the application and preliminary examination

The individual application may be petitioned to the Constitutional Court in person by using the application form or it may be petitioned via other courts (civil and criminal courts), public prosecutor offices or missions in foreign countries. When the application form is submitted, a receipt document is given and the date of such receipt is accepted as the date of application (Article 63 of the Internal Regulations).

Individual application bureau registers the applications submitted to the Court with an application number and oversees the completion of the deficiencies in application if any administrative deficiencies are detected. Fifteen-days extra time shall be allowed for the completion of the deficiencies detected. If the deficiencies are not completed within the time period allowed, then the Chief Rapporteur of the Commissions decides the application to be declared inadmissible on administrative grounds. Such decision of rejection may be challenged within seven days. Such an objection may be concluded by the commissions and the decision rendered upon objection is final (Articles 65 and 66 of the Internal Regulations).

The applications registered and numbered by the individual applications bureau are distributed automatically among the commissions and sections. The applications are examined and concluded in sequence of application date in principle. However, the Court may adopt a different sequence of examination depending on the importance and urgency of the subject matter (Articles 67 and 68 of the Internal Regulations).

C – Examination of admissibility

In order to render a decision on the admissibility of an individual application, all above-examined material and procedural criteria for individual application must be satisfied.

Examination for admissibility is conducted by the commissions. In case a commission decides by unanimous vote that an application does not fulfill requirements for admissibility, the application is declared inadmissible. Application files for which unanimous vote cannot be reached are referred to the Sections.

Sections may dismiss applications which do not bear significance for the enforcement and interpretation of the Constitution, or for the determination of the scope and limits of fundamental rights, applications which do not require meritorious decisions and which do not involve significant damage sustained by the applicant.

In-admissiblity decisions are final and notified to concerned parties. (Article 48 of the CCL).

D – Examination on the merits

According to Article 49 of the CCL, examination of admissible individual applications on the merits is conducted by the Sections. The President takes necessary measures to balance distribution of workload evenly among Sections.

In case an individual application is declared admissible, a copy of the application is notified to the Ministry of Justice. If the Ministry of Justice deems it necessary, it notifies its opinion to the Court in writing[98]. The Ministry of Justice shall provide its opinion within thirty-day

---

98 An annulment action was filed against this provision in Article 49/2 of the CCL on the grounds that the said provision is unconstitutional as it infringes judicial independency, causes suspicion with regards to fair trial and undermine the confidence in the individual application. The application was dismissed with the decision of the Constitutional Court dated 1.3.2012, Nr. E.2011/59, K.2012/34: "*In Article 49 of the said Law, the legislative organ laid down the necessary rules of procedure for the determination of, if any, the violation of right by setting a*

period and this period can be extended by another thirty days upon request. The response of the Ministry of Justice, if any, is notified to the applicant. The applicant may present his/ her counter declarations within fifteen days from the date of notification (Article 71 of the Internal Regulations).

While reviewing the individual applications, commissions and sections may conduct any research and examination so as to determine whether a fundamental right has been violated or not. Information, documents and evidence deemed relevant to the application are requested from the concerned parties. Information and documents submitted to the Court shall be communicated to the applicant and the Ministry of Justice. They shall submit their own opinions, if they deem it necessary to do so, within fifteen days after such communication. If the Court reaches a conclusion that the applicant or public authority refrains from presenting the required information or document or conceals any evidence, or does not attend the trial efficiently in spite of being invited under any circumstances, it renders its judgment drawing the necessary inferences from this situation. (Article 70 of the Internal Regulations).

Sections examine applications on files. However, where considered necessary *ex offico* or upon request of the applicant, or the Ministry of Justice, it can be decided to hold a hearing (Article 74, Paragraph 1 of the Internal Regulations).

The examination to be conducted by the sections with regards to individual applications against to a court decision is restricted with determining whether a fundamental right has been violated and how that violation may be eliminated. Sections do not examine the issues to be considered in the process of an ordinary legal remedy[99].

In the examination of individual applications, provisions of relevant procedural laws which relate to the individual application, especially Code of Civil Procedure Nr.6100, are applied in cases for which no provisions are laid down in this present Law and the Internal Regulation.

---

regulation that the commissions and sections may carry out all types of examinations and investigations when examining individual applicationsso as to determine whether a fundamental right has been violated or not and that they may demand all necessary information, documents and evidences from related parties. Furthermore, the legislative organ stated in the same article that the Court may decide to hold a hearing if it deems necessary to do so, that, may decide for measures they deem necessary and that provisions of relevant procedural laws which relate to the individual application may be applied in cases for which no provisions are laid down in the Law and the Internal Regulation.

In individual application, one of the parties is the "applicant"alleging that his/her right has been violated and the other party is the public authority alleged to have caused the violation of right. In this respect, the individual application differs from the Constitutional justice, in other words from the abstract and concrete norm review. *Therefore, the fact that certain tools of procedural law, such as those subject to annulment action, have been included by the legislative organ among the means of examination to determine a possible violation is a requirement of the fair trial and they cannot be considered as an intervention to the independency of the courts, or an order or directive given to the courts".* :http://www.anayasa.gov.tr/index.php?l= manage_k (date of accession: 22.07.2013).

99 "All issues to be considered in the process of an ordinary legal remedy" are not subject to constitutional complaint. However, all issues within the scope of the constitutional complaint must also be considered in the process of legal remedy." Göztepe – Değerlendirme p. 23; Kanadoğlu, Korkut: Anayasa Şikayeti: HUKAB Sempozyum Serisi 1, 13 Mayıs 2011, p. 109.

E – Temporary injunction

The Sections may, *ex officio* or upon request of the applicant, decide for measures they deem necessary for the protection of the applicant's fundamental rights at the phase of the examination on merits. (Article 49, Paragraph 5 of the CCL). Upon determining that there is a grave danger to the life, or material or spiritual integrity of the applicant, a decision of injunction may be given. In case the Section decides to render an injunction, it communicates it to the concerned people and bodies to take necessary action to execute it (Article 73, Paragraph 3 of the Internal Regulations).

Concerning the applications having been examined; upon seeing that there is a grave danger to the life or material or spiritual integrity of the applicant in case the temporary injunction is not resorted to upon request of the applicant or *ex officio* before deciding on the merits of the case, examination of admissibility of the application is forthwith made by Commissions and the application is referred to the relevant Section so that the issue of measure will be resolved (Article 73, Paragraph 2 of the Internal Regulations).

Decision on the merits of the application about which a temporary injunction has been determined should be given within six months at the latest. When a new decision on continuation of the injunction is not made within this time period, the temporary injunction ceases automatically in case it is decided that the right of the applicant is not violated or the application is dismissed (Article 73, Paragraph 4 of the Internal Regulations).

F – Pilot decision procedure

Although pilot decision method is not proposed in the CCL, it is prescribed in the Internal Regulations (Article 75). In case Sections determine that an application stems from a structural problem and this problem leads to other applications as well, or in case they consider that this situation will lead to new applications, they may apply pilot decision procedure. In this procedure, a pilot decision on the matter is given by the Section. Applications of similar nature are settled within the framework of these principles by administrative authorities; in case they are not settled, they are handled collectively and resolved by the Court.

The Section can initiate the pilot decision procedure *ex offico*, or upon request of the Ministry of Justice or the applicant. The application chosen for execution of the pilot decision is considered among the primary issues of the agenda. The Section, with the pilot decision, may adjourn the examination of similar applications concerning the structural problem discussed in this decision. The concerned people are informed about the resolution for adjournment. The Section may put the applications it has adjourned on the agenda and reach a decision on them in case when considered necessary.

The Section which examines the pilot case on the merits may state, in addition to the ordinary points and issues to be included in the decision, the structural problem that it determined and possible measures to be adopted for the elimination of such structural problem.

G – Decision on the merits

It is regulated in Article 50 of the CCL. After examination on the merits, a decision on violation or non-violation of the applicant's right is rendered by the Sections. In case of a decision on violation, a judgment may be rendered on the actions to be taken in order to abolish the violation and its consequences. However, discretionary review may not be conducted and decisions in the nature of administrative act may not be rendered.

In case the violation has been caused by a court decision, case shall be sent to the (local) court or authority for re-trial in order to erase the violation and its consequences[100]. Accordingly, if the violation is related to a court trial, then this situation may be accepted to be a reason for a new trial as happened for the judgments of the European Court of Human Rights. The relevant court in charge of re-trial holds a re-trial in such a manner that it will remove the infringement and its consequences which the Constitutional Court has explained in its decision of violation, and if possible, decides on the file urgently (Article 79,1-a of the Internal Regulations).

As a result of examination held by Sections, should it be decided that one right of the applicant has been infringed; proper damages could be awarded in favor of the applicant in case no legal benefit is found in holding a re-trial, e.g. long trial periods. In cases where fixing of the amount of damages requires a more detailed examination, e.g. conducting an investigation, expert investigation, on-site viewing etc., the Section could indicate the remedy of filing an action at general courts, without making a decision on this issue itself (Article 79,1- b,c of the Internal Regulations).

The reasoned decisions made by Sections on the merits of the case are notified to the concerned people and the Ministry of Justice. All the decisions made by Sections on the merits of the case and the decisions of Commissions which have importance in principle in terms of admissibility are published on the web site of the Court. Similarly, the decisions which the Section Presidents have determined, which are of nature of pilot decisions made by the Sections or

---

100 An annulment action was filed against this provision in Article 50, Paragraph 2 of the CCL on the grounds that the jurisdiction of the Constitutional Court with regards to individual application is limited to determinig the violation of rights, that the Court can not give orders or instructions to other courts, that the said provision paves the way for such a practice and that such an power can not be granted to the Constitutional Court by enacting a law. The application was dismissed with the decision of the Constitutional Court dated 1.3.2012, Nr. E.2011/59, K.2012/34: *"The individual application remedy, as it is included in Article 148 of the Constitution, is not a case just for the determination of whether a right has been violated or not as it is stated in the petition for annulment action. Individual application is a case which aims to prevent the violation of individuals' fundamental rights and freedoms by the public power and, if a violation is determined, to create legal results which eliminate the results of such violation and compensate the damages sustained. Therefore, the legislative organ included the necessary rules of procedure befitting the nature of the individual application. It is evident that the duty of the Constitutional Court is not limited to just determining the violation of rights and that the Court must be capable of rendering decisions which eliminate such violations.*
Furthermore, there is no rule in Article 148 of the Constitution which states that the duty of the Constitutional Court is limited to just determining the violation of rights as alleged in the petition for annulment action. Legislative power is a general and original power and the legislative organ does not need a special authorization by the Constitutional Court to enact regulations on this issue. Therefore, the legislative organ may make a regulation in any field which is not explicitly prohibited in the Constitution. The regulations included in the rule subject to annulment action must also be assessed in this context". :http://www.anayasa.gov.tr/index.php?l= manage_k (date of accession: 22.07.2013).

which have importance in principle in terms of establishing case law, are published in the Official Gazette (Article 81,3,-5 of the Internal Regulations).

If the decisions made by Sections are contradictory, or if they contain contraversial issues, the concerned persons may request for correction of factual or material errors, and for elucidation of the judgment, within the framework of provisions of the Code of Civil Procedure Nr. 6100 (Article 82 of the Internal Regulations) .

The disparities of judicial opinions between the commissions are resolved by their relevant section and the disparities of judicial opinions between the sections are resolved by the General Assembly.

H – Decision of dismissal

In case of the following cases, decision of dismissal can be made at all stages of trial by Sections or Commissions:

1 – Explicit withdrawal of the applicant from the case,

2 – Understanding that the applicant has dismissed his/ her proceedings,

3 – Termination of infringement and its consequences,

4 – Due to any other justification determined by Sections or Commissions, finding no cause which justifies the continuation of examination of the application.

In cases when the application has constitutional significance, i.e. the application bears significance for the enforcement and interpretation of the Constitution, or for the determination of the scope and limits of fundamental rights, or where respect for human rights requires to do so, Sections or Commissions may continue examining an application of the nature specified in the paragraph above.

I – Abuse of the right of Application

Applicants who are established to have clearly abused the right of individual application with his/ her abusive, misleading behaviors and his/ her behaviors of similar nature, may be required to pay fine not more than 2000 Turkish Liras in addition to the costs and expenses of proceedings and such applications are rejected (Article 51 of the CCL; Article 83 of the Internal Regulations).

References

Aliyev, Cabir: Anayasa Şikayeti, İstanbul 2010.

Armağan, Servet: Federal Almanya'da Anayasa Şikayeti: Mukayeseli Hukuk Araştırmaları Dergisi, C.7, Ayrı Bası, İstanbul 1971.

Atasoy, Hakan: Türk Hukukunda Bireysel Başvuru Yolu: Türkiye Adalet Akademisi Dergisi, Yıl:3, Sayı:9, Nisan 2012, s. 71-98.

Çoban, Ali Rıza: Yeni Anayasa Mahkemesi Kanunu'nun Mahkemenin İş Yüküne Etkisi Açısından Değerlendirilmesi: "Bireysel Başvuru, Anayasa Şikayeti": HUKAB Sempozyum Serisi 1, 13 Mayıs 2011, s. 161-177.

Değnekli, Adnan: Yargıtay'ın Anayasa Şikayetine Bakışı: "Bireysel Başvuru, Anayasa Şikayeti", HUKAB Sempozyum Serisi 1, 13 Mayıs 2011, s. 77-88.

Doğru, Osman: Anayasa Mahkemesine Bireysel Başvuru Rehberi, İstanbul 2012 (Doğru-Bireysel Başvuru).

Doğru, Osman: Anayasa İle Karşılaştırmalı İnsan Hakları Avrupa Sözleşmesi ve Mahkeme İçtüzüğü, İstanbul 2010.

Ekinci, Hüseyin: Anayasa Mahkemesi Kanunu Çerçevesinde Bireysel Başvuruların İncelenme Usulü: "Bireysel Başvuru, Anayasa Şikayeti", HUKAB Sempozyum Serisi 1, 13 Mayıs 2011, s. 137-160.

Ekinci, Hüseyin /Sağlam, Musa: 66 Soruda Anayasa Mahkemesine Bireysel Başvuru, Ankara 2012.

Esen Arnwine, Selin: İspanya'da Amparo Başvurusu ve Türkiye: Anayasa Mahkemesi'ne Bireysel Başvuru Hakkı Sempozyumu, 26 Kasım 2010, Eskişehir 2011, s. 99-115.

Gerçeker, Hasan: Anayasa Mahkemesine Bireysel Başvuru (Anayasa Şikayeti) Konulu Uluslararası Sempozyum Açılış Konuşması: "Bireysel Başvuru, Anayasa Şikayeti": HUKAB Sempozyum Serisi 1, 13 Mayıs 2011, s. 30-36.

Gören, Zafer: Anayasa Şikayeti: Külfetsiz, Masrafsız ve Sonuçsuz ?: Prof. Dr. Ergun Özbudun'a Armağan, Cilt II, Ankara 2008, s. 293-337.

Görgün, Emin /Aydın, Yakup: Sayıştay Kararlarına Karşı Anayasa Mahkemesine Bireysel Başvuru Yolu: Sayıştay Dergisi, Yıl 2012, Sayı:84, s. 63-88.

Gözler Kemal: Türk Anayasa Hukuku Dersleri, 9.B, Bursa 2010.

Gözler, Kemal: İdare Hukuku Dersleri, 10. B., Bursa 2010.

Göztepe, Ece: Anayasa Şikayeti, Anakara 1998, (Göztepe-Şikayet)

Göztepe Ece: Türkiye'de Anayasa Mahkemesi'ne Bireysel Başvuru Hakkının (Anayasa Şikayeti) 6216 Sayılı Kanun Kapsamında Değerlendirilmesi: Türkiye Barolar Birliği Dergisi 2011 (95), s. 13-40. (Göztepe – Değerlendirme)

Kanadoğlu, Korkut: Anayasa Şikayeti: HUKAB Sempozyum Serisi 1, Bireysel Başvuru "Anayasa Şikayeti" Ankara 2011, s. 107-115.

Kılınç, Bahadır: Federal Almanya'da Bireysel Başvuru (Anayasa Şikayeti) Yolu:Anayasa Mahkemesi'ne Bireysel Başvuru Hakkı Sempozyumu, 26 Kasım 2010, Eskişehir 2011, s. 87. (s. 87-98).

Kuru, Baki / Arslan, Ramazan /Yılmaz, Ejder: Medenî Usul Hukuku Ders Kitabı, 22.B., Ankara 2011.

Kuru, Baki / Arslan, Ramazan /Yılmaz, Ejder: İcra ve İflâs Hukuku Ders Kitabı, 24. B., Ankara 2010.

Mellinghof, Rudolf: Federal Almanya Cumhuriyetinde Anayasa Şikayeti: Anayasa Yargısı, C.26, 2009, s. 31-44.

Oder, Bertil Emrah: Anayasa Mahkemesine Bireysel Başvuruda (Anayasa Şikayeti) Etkin ve Etkili Kullanım Sorunları: HUKAB Sempozyum Serisi 1, Bireysel Başvuru "Anayasa Şikayeti" Ankara 2011, s. 89 – 106.

Öcal, Saniye: Die Einführung der Verfassungsbeschwerde Als Neues Recht In der Türkei: Eine Besserstellung zum Schutz der Grund- Freiheitsrechte ? : Yedi Tepe Üniversitesi Hukuk Fakültesi Dergisi, C.VII/1, 2010, s. 214.

Özbey, Özcan: Türk Hukukunda Anayasa Mahkemesine Bireysel Başvuru, 2. B., Ankara 2013.

Pekcanıtez, Hakan: Mukayeseli Hukukta Medeni Yargıda Verilen Kararlara Karşı Anayasa Şikayeti: Anayasa Yargısı 12, Ankara 1995, s. 257-287.

Pekcanıtez, Hakan: İcra – İflâs Hukukunda Şikayet, Ankara 1986.

Pekcanıtez, Hakan / Atalay, Oğuz / Özekes, Muhammet: Medenî Usul Hukuku, 12. B., Ankara 2011.

Sabuncu, Yavuz / Arnwine Esen, Selin: Türkiye İçin Anayasa Şikayeti Model, Türkiye'de Bireysel Başvuru Yolu: Anayasa Yargısı, C.21, 2004, s. 229-246.

Sağlam, Fazıl: Anayasa Şikayeti Kurumunun Türk Hukukuna Kazandırılması ile İlgili Sorunlar ve Çözüm Olanakları: Anayasa Yargısı İncelemeleri 1, Ankara 2006, s. 71- 111. (F. Sağlam – Anayasa Şikayeti)

Sağlam, Fazıl: Anayasa Mahkemesinin 47. Kuruluş Yıldönümü Nedeniyle Düzenlenen "Bireysel Başvuru ve Dünyadaki Uygulaması" Konulu Sempozyum; Giriş ve Takdim Konuşması: Anayasa Yargısı 2009, Sayı 26, s. 27. (F. Sağlam –Konuşma)

Sağlam, Fazıl: Anayasa Şikayeti Anlamı, Kapsamı ve Türkiye Uygulamasında Olası Sorunlar: Demokratik Anayasa (Görüşler Öneriler), Editör: Aykut Çelebi, Ece Göztepe, Ankara 2011, s. 430-431.

Sağlam, Musa: Bir Hak Arama Yolu Olarak Bireysel Başvuru: Anayasa Mahkemesi'ne Bireysel Başvuru Hakkı Sempozyumu, 26 Kasım 2010, Eskişehir 2011, s. 14-64, (Sağlam – Bireysel Başvuru).

Sağlam, Musa: 1982 Anayasası ve 6216 Sayılı Kanun Çerçevesinde Bireysel Başvuru Konusu Haklar: Anayasa Mahkemesinin Kuruluşunun 50. Yılına Armağan, Ankara 2012, s. 267-307, (Sağlam – Haklar).

Tercan, Erdal: Medeni Usul Hukukunda Kesin Sürelerin Kaçırılması Halinde Eski Hale Getirme, Ankara 2006.

Tercan, Erdal /Tercan Süheyla: İcra ve İflâs Hukuku, Ankara 2005.

Teziç, Erdoğan: Parlamento Kararı ve Kanun: Anayasa Yargısı, C.5, 1989, s. 121-130.

Tülen, Hikmet: Anayasa Mahkemesinin Yeniden Yapılandırılmasına İlişkin Anayasa Değişikliği Taslağı Üzerine Açıklamalar ve Birkaç Öneri, http.//www.e-akademi.org/makaleler/htulen-1.htm (erişim tarihi: 16.07.2013).